THE SCOTTISH CLASSICS SERIES

NUMBER TWO

THE MEMBER: AN AUTOBIOGRAPHY

THE SCOTTISH CLASSICS SERIES

GENERAL EDITOR — DOUGLAS S. MACK

JOHN GALT

THE MEMBER:
An Autobiography

EDITED BY
IAN A. GORDON

SCOTTISH ACADEMIC PRESS
in association with
THE ASSOCIATION FOR SCOTTISH LITERARY STUDIES
EDINBURGH
1985

Published by
Scottish Academic Press Ltd
25 Perth Street, Edinburgh 3
and distributed by
Chatto & Windus Ltd
40 William IV Street
London W.C.2

First published 1975
SBN 7011 2084 3

Introduction and Notes
© 1975 Ian A. Gordon

Galt, John
    John Galt : the member - an autobiography.
    1. Galt, John   2. Authors, Scottish——19th
    century——Biography
    I. Title   II. Gordon, Ian A.
    823'.7   PR4708.G2Z/

    ISBN 0-7073-0464-4

Printed in Great Britain by
Billing & Sons, Worcester

CONTENTS

v

INTRODUCTION

I

John Galt wrote *The Member* in 1831. The author for some years had been enduring a frustrating lack of success in all his ventures and need had driven him to produce a series of hack novels that was giving him no great reason for pride. *The Member* of 1831, a return to an earlier and successful genre, was an almost symbolic reaffirmation of his original creative powers.

Galt[1] at the age of forty, after a career as business-man, parliamentary agent, journalist, fabricator of books of travel and school textbooks, emerged into the world of literature with the appearance of *The Ayrshire Legatees* in 1820. Thereafter, till 1826, a series of Scots novels, that included in rapid succession *Annals of the Parish*, *The Provost*, *The Entail*, and *The Last of the Lairds*, brought him both financial reward and a firm reputation. He was well received by the critical journals of the day and Coleridge, on reading *The Entail* and *The Provost*, placed him 'in the front rank of contemporary novelists'.

Galt, however, had always nourished a private dream of exercising power in the world of affairs, and in 1826 gave up novel-writing for a position, with the Canada Company, as Superintendent of Upper Canada. Less than three years later the dream of power was over. He was recalled to England, his position with the Company at an end, and his alarmed creditors closing in on him. He found himself in the debtors' prison of the King's Bench, where he doggedly resumed his writing, grinding out for the firm of Colburn and Bentley the first of what was to become a succession of three-volume novels. Galt disliked the three-volume format that the circulating libraries of his day demanded, and he had no illusions about his publishers who, as he recorded, gave him orders for novels 'like to an upholsterer for a piece of furniture'. But the income from his regular pieces in *Blackwood's Magazine* and *Fraser's Magazine* was inadequate, and he continued to write commissioned books for Colburn and Bentley till 1832, noting grimly in his later *Literary Life* that 'he would not wish to be estimated by them'. Meantime he bided his time, till he could write something more congenial.

The opportunity came in the latter part of 1831, when his fortunes took a turn for the better. Galt was appointed secretary of the British American Land Company, and with the prospect of a regular income came escape from working to order like an upholsterer. He saw his way to write once again a book in a format and on a theme of his own choosing, in which (to use his own words) 'what was lost in popularity would be made up in durability'. Galt knew that his best literary work had always been done in a single short volume and in the 'autobiographical' genre that he had mastered in *Annals of the Parish* and *The Provost*. He completed *The Member* rapidly and it was published, in January 1832, by James Fraser, the proprietor of *Fraser's Magazine*. With it, Galt escaped from the treadmill of Colburn and Bentley, producing yet another little masterpiece of ironical self-revelation, his new hero Archibald Jobbry taking his place immediately alongside the Reverend Micah Balwhidder and Provost Pawkie. Even the title-page of the new book indicated Galt's escape. The enforced author had been signing his recent Colburn and Bentley productions as 'by John Galt'. *The Member* bore no author's name; it did not require one. It was simply 'by the author of "The Ayrshire Legatees", etc. etc.' The message was understood – we wish, wrote *The Athenaeum* on 28 January, that 'Mr Galt would write nothing but imaginary autobiographies'. The other contemporary reviewers were equally enthusiastic.

Galt had always been fascinated by the theory and the practice of political power. As a young man he had read Machiavelli and had written on him as far back as 1814. He had then successfully tackled the theme in fiction: Mr Pawkie, the central figure of *The Provost* (begun in 1821), is a small-town politician, a shrewd manipulator of men and events, fitted for an assembly larger than the mere Town Council of a small borough. It was to the larger assembly of Westminster that Galt now turned his mind. He had an extensive knowledge of Parliament. For many years he had been a parliamentary agent, lobbying for a variety of Scottish and Canadian interests. He was not uniformly successful; he contrived to shepherd several Scottish private bills through the House; his efforts on behalf of his Canadian clients were in the end fruitless. But in the course of these protracted negotiations he had learned how the mechanism of government operated. He knew dozens of members and key cabinet ministers. He had seen from the inside the workings of the old unreformed House, knew the system of balances of pressures and patronage, of private and public interest, on which the practical manipulation of government was based. He knew at first hand how the ordinary member of parliament had to think and act if he were to survive and succeed.

In the course of his fraternisation with members, he acquired an encyclopedic knowledge of the operation of the franchise. Before 1832, voting rights in the constituencies represented a series of diversified historical survivals, each jealously preserved. There were multiple routes to Parliament.[2] A member could be openly elected (almost in the modern sense) if he tried for a populous London seat and had to appeal to its thousands of voters; he could (on the other hand) be elected by a tiny handful, in a county or corporation constituency where votes were in the patronage of a local landowner; he could sit for a 'rotten' borough, where 'election' was reduced to a formality; he could even gain his seat by an outright – even if it had to be discreet – cash payment. Galt was well aware of the ironical possibilities and he made full use of his knowledge in *The Member*.

His hero, Archibald Jobbry, surveys these possibilities and decides on outright purchase. His target is Frailtown. Galt is always at his best when he bases his fiction on fact, and his instinct did not desert him. A careful reading of the text reveals that he had a real constituency in mind. Frailtown is (chapter vii) in 'Vamptonshire', which phonetically suggests Northamptonshire. It is (chapter xiii) somewhat beyond a reasonable night and day chaise journey (i.e. about 50 miles) 'on the north road' from London – Jobbry and his agent put up at 'Beverington', a few miles short of their goal. Frailtown (chapter vii) is within a few miles of 'Physickspring', a thriving spa. It is portrayed as a 'corporation' borough, and returns one member to Parliament. Only one place in England in the period satisfies all these conditions. Higham Ferrers in Northamptonshire is 64 miles from London. It is about five miles from Wellingborough, once a famous spa. It was best approached by 'the north road' through St Albans; and Bedford (51 miles from London), with three inns that supplied post horses for the onward journey, was an obvious stopover. There seems little doubt that Bedford, Wellingborough and the corporation one-member borough of Higham Ferrers provided Galt with his models for Beverington, Physickspring, and the corporation one-member borough of Frailtown.

Galt, to heighten the irony, has reduced the number of voters in Frailtown to six. The actuality was not so very far different. The franchise of Higham Ferrers[3] (before it disappeared with other doomed boroughs in Schedule A of the Act of 1832) was in the hands of the corporation – which consisted of the Mayor (who was also the returning officer), seven aldermen, thirteen Capital Burgesses, plus 'freemen, being householders, not receiving alms', these latter in a permanent minority, since the total electorate did not exceed 40. Galt's only slightly exaggerated picture of oligarchic control is deadly in its essential accuracy.

Galt's verisimilitude went even further. Like Mr Galore in *The Provost* and Mr Rupees in *The Last of the Lairds*, Archibald Jobbry is a Scot, returned wealthy from service in Bengal with the East India Company. The man who for years dominated the Company's Board of Control was the Edinburgh lawyer-politician, Viscount Melville, who was openly – and accurately – accused of filling British India with Scotsmen; and the Company ensured that its servants on their retirement from India were returned in substantial numbers to the House of Commons.[4] There is no evidence that Galt had a specific model for his Mr Jobbry, as he had for his Mr Pawkie. But the Scots nabob M.P. (sitting for an English constituency, where back-door entry by purchase was easy) was a familiar figure in the corridors of Westminster and a clear candidate for ironical portrayal.

2

The Member is thus an accurately-observed study of the operation of political power in the years before the passing of the Reform Bill of 1832. It is a novel, not a treatise in political science, the first political novel in English. Structurally, it has the characteristics of all the best Galt novels, which Galt himself called his 'theoretical histories of society'. Galt selects a theme and a protagonist, who is set to recount his own narrative in annalistic or chronicle form. There is no 'plot', simply a succession of what (on the surface at least) are apparently unrelated scenes and incidents. There is, however, nothing haphazard or inconsequential in Galt's choice of his narrative material. In each scene or incident, the protagonist reveals yet another facet of his personality, and unity and shape are impressed on the whole annalistic sequence by Galt's controlling ironical presentation. The unity that finally emerges from *Annals of the Parish*, *The Provost*, and *The Member* is a unity of tone and attitude.

The Member is a single volume of thirty-six chapters. Though there are no physical indications, it falls into three clearly defined sections. In the first section (chapters i–xvii) Archibald Jobbry is on the upward path. In the early chapters, he decides to enter Parliament, his motive being entirely self-interest. He has returned wealthy from Bengal and bought an estate in Scotland. But he is surrounded by humble relations 'gaping like voracious larks' for patronage. He drives a canny bargain over the purchase of the seat of Frailtown (in a series of scenes of high comedy) and enters Parliament 'to make power for myself', more specifically (as he freely admits), 'to help my kith and kin by a judicious assistance to Government'. He revels in the role of dispenser of patronage to relations and constituents, and even more in the manipulation of ministers which it entails. By the end of his second session he is a toughened veteran, able to meet the challenge of an unexpected rival candidate, and Galt presents in chapters xiii–xv a riotous picture of a contested election in the thoroughly corrupt borough of Frailtown. Jobbry is returned by his own efforts, without benefit of the local patron, and his new independence gives him a powerful lever when he bargains with ministers for further patronage and has to survive – as he does triumphantly – a change of ministry. His jaunty self-assurance is that of a born survivor.

In the second section (chapters xviii–xxviii) the tone alters. The opening two chapters (xviii, xix) form the turning-point of the novel. Jobbry attempts to take up the grievances of Mr Selby, who has suffered at the hands of Government (Galt here draws on his own experiences in handling the claims of his Canadian clients, whose plight had been that of Mr Selby). Jobbry is brought to doubt the system he has been exploiting so triumphantly – 'my opinions underwent a change' – with the result that the offended patron of 'his' borough puts up a candidate against him. But Jobbry survives once again in yet another riotous election and was 'a second time *elected* [the ironical italics are Galt's] the independent representative of Frailtown'. But the case of Mr Selby still troubles him and he finds on his return to Parliament he had 'lost something of my relish' for the manipulation of favours. A 'moderate Tory', he cannot in honesty deny all the claims of the reformers, and an encounter with the now destitute family of Mr Selby so disturbs him that his breakfast 'Findhorn haddock was sent away untasted'. When he humanely arranges a better future for the destitute children, a new Mr Jobbry has emerged.

The final section (chapters xxix–xxxvi) is largely taken up with the issues of the day, the Money Question, the Corn Laws, the Catholic Relief Bill (which Jobbry supports). Much as he dislikes the Radicals, he finds himself out of sympathy with the 'real Tories of the House', who were against any change – 'These I looked on as the pillars of the state; but I was not myself one of them.' What would appear to be his final change of heart comes when he is invited to the country. Disaffected agricultural labourers set a farm on fire, and the military are called out. Mr Jobbry, watching the incident among the spectators, is arrested, bound, thrown on a cart, and brought before an irate magistrate, who half-strangles him before his identity is discovered. Jobbry has been forced to discover what it is like to be without privilege, and he reflects on the incident sadly: it would have been more creditable to the justices, instead of 'scouring the country with dragoons', to have met in council and considered soberly 'the complaints of the people'. The 'moderate Tory' realises that the Reformers will win the day and he decides the time has come for him to retire from Parliament and sell his seat.

But Galt's irony never flags. The borough of Frailtown is unsaleable; it is listed on the Schedule of doomed constituencies in the Reform Act. The chastened Mr Jobbry has to retreat to his Scottish estate 'as a simple spectator' and – away from it all, his transitory liberalism rapidly fading – he dedicates his autobiography in true-blue language and style to his old friend, the chief Tory whip. Leopards, Galt implies, in this delightfully cyclic conclusion, never really change their spots.

3

The later history of *The Member* is curiously like Mr Jobbry's. It, too, simply faded from sight. The novel was excellently reviewed on its appearance, both in England and on the Continent, but James Fraser, the publisher, seemed to have lacked the skill required for book promotion. He produced and sold a popular monthly magazine; he had no expertise in the book-trade. A book needs more than an author. Colburn and Bentley, with their aggressive methods, were able to sell two large editions of Galt's much inferior *Lawrie Todd*, and part of their run of the second edition even appeared in distant Australia, with a new title-page and a Melbourne imprint. Meanwhile, William Blackwood in Edinburgh held the copyrights of all of Galt's best known novels: *The Ayrshire Legatees, Annals of the Parish, Sir Andrew Wylie, The Provost, The Entail, The Last of the Lairds*. The firm saw no reason for buying in any other copyrights, and on Galt's death these six novels appeared and were several times reprinted in 'Blackwood's Standard Novels'. Subsequently, they were again reprinted as a uniform set unequivocally entitled 'The Works of John Galt'. *The Member* had simply dropped out of sight, a casualty of publishing history.[5] Galt had intended it to stand alongside his earlier 'theoretical histories' as a companion piece, written on his own terms and (in his own phrase) 'con amore'. It is now presented, after a lapse of nearly a century and a half, as a work that merits attention both as a social document and as a lively and well-written novel. I have provided the full annotation that a 'period' novel now requires, and a short glossary. The text is derived from a xerox of the British Museum copy. I am grateful to Godfrey Thompson, F.L.A., City of London librarian, for information from the archives of the Guildhall Library.

Wellington, 1973   I.A.G.

1. For all citations on Galt and for a bibliography see Ian A. Gordon, *John Galt The Life of a Writer*, 1972.
2. For the full complexity of the franchise see E. Porrit, *The Unreformed House of Commons*, 2 vols., 1903.
3. *Higham Ferrers*: see T. H. B. Oldfield, *The Representative History of Great Britain* (6 vols., 1816), vol. ii, pp. 292–5.
4. C. H. Philips, *The East India Company*, 1940, p. 5, and Appendix I.
5. *The Member* was published in January 1832. A one-volume sequel *The Radical* was published by Fraser in May. The unsold sheets of both were made up into a single volume, entitled *The Reform*, issued in November.

DEDICATION

WILLIAM HOLMES, Esq. M.P.

The Girlands, Jan. 1, 1832.

MY DEAR SIR,

I beg leave to inscribe to you this brief Memoir of my parliamentary services, and I do so on the same principle that our acquaintance, Colonel Napier, refers to as his motive in dedicating that interesting work, the History of the Peninsular War, to the Duke of Wellington. It was chiefly under your kind superintendence that I had the satisfaction of exerting myself as an independent member, really and cordially devoted to the public good, during many anxious campaigns; and now, retired for ever from the busy scene, it is natural that I should feel a certain satisfaction in associating your respected name with this humble record.

If the Reform Bill passes, which an offended Providence seems, I fear, but too likely to permit, your own far more brilliant and distinguished career as a patriotic senator is, probably, also drawing to a conclusion; and withdrawn, like me, to a rural retreat, in the calm repose of an evening hour, no longer liable to sudden interruption, it may serve to amuse your leisure to cast an eye over the unpretending narrative of scenes and events so intimately connected in my mind with the recollection of your talents, zeal, and genius, in what, though not generally so considered by the unthinking mass, I have long esteemed nearly the most important situation which any British subject can fill; but which, alas! is perhaps destined to pass away and be forgotten, amidst this general convulsion so fatal to the established institutions of a once happy and contented country. If, indeed, my dear and worthy friend, the present horrid measure be carried into full effect, it is but too plain that the axe will have been laid to the root of the British Oak. The upsetting, short-sighted conceit of new-fangled theorems will not long endure either the aristocratic or the monarchic branches; and your old office, so useful and necessary even, under a well-regulated social system, will fall with the rest; for the sharp, dogged persons likely to be returned under the schedules, will need no remembrancer to call

I

them to their congenial daily and nightly task of retrenchment and demolition.

A melancholy vista discloses itself to all rational understandings; – a church in tatters; a peerage humbled and degraded – no doubt, soon to be entirely got rid of; that poor, deluded man, the well-meaning William IV, probably packed off to Hanover; the three per cents down to two, at the very best of it; a graduated property tax sapping the vitals of order in all quarters; and, no question, parliamentary grants and pensions of every description no longer held sacred!

May you be strengthened to endure with firmness the evil day; and if the neighbourhood of London should become so disturbed as to render Fulham no more that sweet snug retirement I always considered it, sure am I, that by making my little sequestered place here your temporary abode during the raging of the storm, you would confer much real pleasure and honour on myself and family. We have capital fishing, both trout and salmon, close at hand; and the moors are well enough all about us, – what with blackcock, grouse, ptarmigan, and occasionally roes, of which the duke's woods near harbour many. Here we might watch afar off the rolling of the popular billows, and the howlings of the wind of change and perturbation, and bide our time.

Once more, dear Mr Holmes, accept the sincere tribute of esteem and regard from your old friend and pupil, and humble servant at command,

ARCHIBALD JOBBRY

P.S. Herewith you will receive 4 brace moorfowl, 2 ditto B. cocks, item 3 hares, one side of a roe, and one gallon whisky (*véritable antique*); which liberty please pardon.

Jan. 2.—I am credibly informed that the weavers of Guttershiels, over their cups on hogmanae and yesterday, were openly discussing the division of landed properties in this district! What have not these demented ministers to answer for?

THE MEMBER

CHAPTER I

When a man comes home from India with a decent competency, he is obliged to endure many afflictions, not the least of which are nestsful of cousins' children, in every corner of the kingdom, all gaping like voracious larks for a pick. This it behoves him to consider; for his bit gathering would be short in the outcoming, were he to help them from that fund: he is therefore under the necessity of reflecting how a modicum of his means can be laid out to the best advantage, not only for the benefit of his relations, but to spare a residue to himself, and to procure for him a suitable station in the world – the end of all creditable industry.

For a time, after I set my foot on my native land, I was troubled in mind with these considerations; for when I left Bengal, it was with an intent to buy a moderate estate, and to live at my ease, having every thing comfortable about me.

Of course, I had no insurmountable difficulty in meeting with a commodious purchase, though maybe I paid the price; for I had to bid against both a paper-money banker and a purse-proud fozy cotton manufacturer. I did not, however, grudge it; for I had the where-withal, and I had seen enough of the world, in the intelligent circles of Calcutta, to convince me that rural felicity had, like many other things, risen in value.

But no sooner was I enfeoft in my property, than my kith and kin began to bestir themselves, and to plague me for my patronage; plead-ing, in a very wearisome manner, that blood was thicker than water. Partly to get quit of their importunities, and to get also the means to help them, I began to take shares in divers public concerns, and to busy myself in the management thereof, slipping in a young friend now and then as a clerk. I will not, however, say, that in this I was altogether actuated by affection; for public spirit had quite as much to say with me as a regard for my kindred: indeed, it is a thing expected of every

3

man, when he retires from business, that he will do his endeavour to serve his country, and make himself a name in the community.

These doings, however, I soon saw were not enough to satisfy the demands upon me; finding, therefore, as I read the newspapers, that I had made myself very passably acquainted, while in India, with the politics of Europe, and especially with the arcana of government and the principles of legislation in England, I began to clok on the idea of getting myself made a Member of Parliament. At first I cannot say that I was strongly thereunto inclined – it was only a hankering; but the more I reflected anent the same, I grew the more courageous, especially when I read the speeches of those that had but speech-making to recommend them. To be sure, there were in my neighbourhood several old lairds, that counted their descent from Adam's elder brother, who, when they heard that I was minded to go into Parliament, snorted east and west, and thought it a most upsetting audacity. But I had not been risking my health for five-and-twenty years in the climate of Bengal to pleasure them; so when I heard how they looked, and what they said concerning me, I became the more obstinate in my intention. But it was not so easily accomplished as thought; for as we in Scotland are not so clever in the way of getting into Parliament, without family connexions, as they are in England, I considered with myself that it would be expedient to take a run up to London when Parliament was sitting, and have some conversation there with a few of my old Indian cronies who were already members.

I could not, however, just go off at once, without giving some reason; for it was then only a five-year old Parliament, and it would not have been prudent to have been thought guilty of looking so long before me as two years, unless there was some prospect of a change in the administration. But it happened that, from the first time I looked at my estate, I saw that the mansion-house stood in need of divers repairs; and accordingly I, in a quiet way, set about getting plans and estimates of the alterations. When I had procured and considered of the same, I instructed a carpenter thereon; and I took the opportunity, when the house was in the cholera morbus of reparation, to set out for London, giving it out that I had old Indian affairs to wind up, and heavy accounts to settle.

It may be thought that I was a little overly artificial in this matter; but I had learned in my experience that no business of this world is without its craft, more especially undertakings of a political nature.

4

Thus it came to pass that I arrived in the dead of winter in London, and was not long of making my arrival known among my acquaintance, and particularly those who had gotten themselves seats. I likewise peutered, in a far-off manner, among the Indian directors, and those that make speeches at their public meetings when the fault-finders give them trouble; still keeping my eye on the main chance.

CHAPTER II

The first of my old acquaintance whom I fell in with was Mr Curry. He had been home from India three years before me, and was in all things a most orderly man. We were right glad, as you may well think, to see one another; and yet there was between us a cool distinction. His business in Calcutta was not just of such a genteel order as mine, but it was a shade more profitable; and hence, though he was a year behind me in the outgoing, he was full three years before me in the home-coming, which shews the difference that was between our respective ways of business; for, in comparing one thing with another, I found that our fortunes were counted just about equal, – which is a proof of the correctness of what I say.

He had heard of my coming home, and likewise how I had made myself a public, patriotic character, which he never thought could happen; and, from less to more, I said to him that I was glad of an employment, for the time hung heavy upon my hands, and 'that if I did not take a share in projects for the good of the nation, I would be indeed a waif hand.'

He remarked to me, that what I said was very true, and consistent with his own experience; 'But I would advise you,' said he, 'to do as I have done; get yourself elected into Parliament – it will not cost you a deadly sum; and then you'll have full occupation.'

'Mr Curry,' quo' I, 'it's not every one, like you, that has a talent; for although I would not grudge to pay for the admission-ticket, between ourselves, I really don't know how to set about applying for one; for you know that in our county in Scotland, the pedigree-family "bear the bell" in all electioneerings; for my Lord Entail, their cousin, has made as many freeholders on the list as the valuation of his estate allows, and three of the district-boroughs are under his thumb; so by that means they have all the rule and power of the shire. But, Mr Curry, if ye could tell me of a sober, canny way of creeping into the House of Commons unobserved, I'll no say that just for a diversion I would not like to sit there for a session or two; by that time I would have made myself joke-fellow like with some of the big-wigs, the which would

6

help to make this country not so disagreeable after the sprees and merry-go-rounds of "auld lang syne" in India.'

'I discern,' said Mr Curry, 'that ye're in the same state of sin and misery that I suffered myself when I came home; and therefore I say unto you, speaking from the knowledge of my own insight, get into Parliament: at the very utmost, Mr Jobbry,' said he, 'a few thousand pounds at a general election should do the business; or, if you would sooner take your seat, I should think that from twelve hundred to fifteen hundred pounds per session would be reasonable terms; for I would not advise you to be overly greedy of a bargain, nor overly logive at the outset.'

I agreed with him that his remark was very judicious, but that really I had no confidential acquaintance in the line; and that it was not to be expected I could, going out to India a bare lad, with scarcely shoon upon my cloots, be in a condition to set myself forward.

'Oh,' says he, 'nothing is more easy; ye have just to give an inkling that if a convenient borough was to be had, ye would not mind about going into Parliament. Speeches of that sort are very efficacious; and it's not to be told how it will circulate that you would give a handsome price for an easy seat in the House of Commons. Keep your thumb on the price, and just let out that you have no relish for the clanjamfrey of a popular election, but would rather deal with an old sneck-drawer in the trade than plague yourself with canvassing: depend upon it ye'll soon hear of some needful lord that will find you out, and a way of treating with you.'

There was certainly sterling admonition in this; and I said to him, over our wine, for we were then sitting together after dinner, in Ibbotson's Hotel, 'that I was not particular in wishing to conceal my hankering for a seat in Parliament.'

'Do you really say so?' said he.

I then assured him that I was not vehemently against it; and so, from less to more, he inquired of what party I would be; and I told him with the government party, to be sure.

'I'll no just say,' quo' he, 'that you are far wrong in your determination, because the Tories have the ball at their foot, and are likely to rule the roast for some years.'

'I daresay they are,' said I; 'but between Whigs and Tories I can make no distinction, – a Tory is but a Whig in office, and a Whig but a Tory in opposition, which makes it not difficult for a conscientious man to support the government.'

7

'Really, Mr Jobbry,' said Mr Curry, 'ye were always thought a far-sighted man, that could see as well through a nether millstone as another man through a stone wall; and, without complimenting you, I must say that you entertain very creditable notions of government, not to be yet a member. But, Mr Jobbry, we are talking in confidence, and what we say to one another is not to be repeated.'

I assured Mr Curry, with the greatest sincerity, that what he told me anent the diplomaticals should never go farther; then, said Mr Curry, in a sedate, sober manner,

'I know a solicitor that has a borough that wants a member, the politics of which are of a delicate tint, you understand; now, I could wise him to you, and you might consult him, – or rather, would it not be better that ye would appoint some friend to confabble with the man?'

'Would not you do that for me?' said I.

'No, no,' said he, 'I'm a member myself, and that would not be playing the game according to Hoyle.'

'Very well,' said I; 'but as I have a great inclination on all occasions to be my own executioner, ye might pass me off with the man as the friend of a gentleman that's wishing to get into Parliament.'

'That's a capital device,' said he; 'and if you draw well together, the cost of an agent and the hazard of a witness may be saved.'

So, thereupon, it was agreed between us that he should speak on the subject to Mr Probe the solicitor, and that I should enact towards that gentleman the representative of my friend, that was to be nameless until the bargain was concluded.

CHAPTER III

Next morning I had occasion to be forth at an early hour, to see some of my old friends at the Jerusalem, concerning a ballot that was that day to take place at the India House; and thus it came to pass, that before I got back to the hotel, a gentleman had called upon me, and not finding me at home, left his card, which was that of Mr Probe the solicitor. I at first did not recollect the name, for it had been only once mentioned; but the waiter told me he would call again in the evening, having some particular private business to transact.

This intimation put me upon my guard, and then recollecting his name, I guessed the errand he had come upon, and told the waiter to prepare for us a private parlour; but in the meantime I would take my dinner in the public coffee-room.

The waiter, being an expert young man, ordered all things in a very perfect manner; and I had just finished my dinner when in came Mr Probe; a smaller sort of man, with a costive and crimson countenance, sharp eyes, and cheeks smooth and well-stuffed: but one thing I remarked about him which I did not greatly admire, and yet could not say wherefore, namely, he had a black fore-tooth, as if addicted to the tobacco-pipe; and, moreover, although it could not be said that he was a corpulent man, he certainly was in a degree one of the fatties; but he was very polite and introductory, told me his name, how Mr Curry had requested him to call, and was, in every respect, as couthy and pleasant as an evil spirit.

I desired the waiter to shew us up into the private room that was ordered, and bade him bring a bottle of Carbonnel's claret – all which he soon did; and when Mr Probe and I were comfortably seated, he opened the business.

'Mr Jobbry,' said he, 'our mutual friend, and my client, has told me that you might have some business in my way.'

'My client!' quo' I to myself, – 'mum,' and then I continued – 'He is an old friend of mine, and I was telling him that the time hung heavy upon my hands in the country—— Oh! but that is not what I wished to speak to you about. I have a particular friend lately come from

India, who is in the same condition: it's far from my fortune, Mr Probe, to think of going into Parliament; but my friend, who has a turn for public speaking, requested me, as I was coming to London, to see if a seat could be obtained on reasonable terms; and speaking on this subject to our mutual friend, Mr Curry (I took care to say nothing of his client), he told me that you had a seat to dispose of, and that he would send you to me.'

'Very correct,' replied Mr Probe; 'but he made a little mistake – I have not a seat to dispose of; but a particular friend told me that he knew of one; and now I recollect of having once mentioned the subject to Mr Curry.'

'It's very right to be guarded,' Mr Probe,' said I, 'especially since the sales of seats in Parliament are as plain as the sun at noon-day, and would make the bones of our ancestors rattle in their coffins to hear of it: but although a seat may be come at by good handling, what would you, just in common parlance, think a fair——

'Oh, Mr. Jobbry, we need not condescend on particulars; but my friend has certainly a capital sporting manor, and will either let it on lease for the remainder of his term, or for an annual rent.'

I patted the side of my nose with my forefinger, and said, in the jocular words of Burns,

'But Tam kent what was what fu' brauly;'

and added, 'Very well, Mr Probe, that's a very judicious alternative; but what's—— I'll not say what. Would it be expected that my friend would have to sit on the right or left hand of a man in a wig; or, in other words, to come to the point, would he have to be a sheep or a goat, for at present he's an innocent lambkin, and unless there be a reason for it, he would naturally be a sheep. I'll no say that he'll ever be a battering-ram; but you understand, Mr Probe?'

'Your candour,' was the reply, 'is exceedingly satisfactory; but have you any notion of what your friend would give for the manor?'

'I doubt,' said I, 'if he will come up to what our friend Curry said was the price.'

'What did he say?' inquired Mr Probe.

'Really I can't tell, – I don't recollect exactly, whether it was three or four thousand pounds.'

'Not possible,' exclaimed the solicitor, falling back in his chair with astonishment.

'Oh,' replied I, 'it is very probable that I am in the wrong, now when I recollect that Parliament has only two sessions to run: you are very right, he could never have said so much as three or four thousand pounds – he must have been speaking of the price of a whole Parliament.'

'Excuse me, Mr Jobbry, you misunderstood him, – either three or four thousand pounds was quite ridiculous to mention in the same breath with a whole Parliament: no, sir, the price that I am instructed to arrange is for the two remaining sessions.'

'Pray, Mr Probe, is the gentleman in the House?'

'He is, but he does not find it suit; and, between ourselves, although money is no object to him, he somehow has not felt himself at home, and so he has a mind to retire.'

'Ay, he has, eh? did he ever say why, because that is a subject that my friend should consider?'

'No, not particularly; but every man who thinks himself qualified does not find himself so, I imagine, when he once gets in.'

'Then, if I understand you, Mr Probe, your client——'

'Not my client!'

'Well, well; he wants, as I understand you, to dispose of the shooting for two years at an annual rent.'

'Just so.'

'And what may he expect, to make few words about it?'

'A couple of thousand.'

'What! for two years?'

'No, not so: two thousand for the first year, and two thousand for the next, – four thousand in all, if the humbug lasts so long.'

'Is that the name of the manor, Mr Probe?'

'Ah! you're a wag, Mr Jobbry.'

'But one serious word, Mr Probe: I am sure my friend will give no such price as two thousand pounds per session, – he only wants the seat for recreation: some people like horses, some hounds, some carriages, some one thing, and some another; and my friend's taste is a seat in the senate; but he is a prudent man – he looks to both sides of the shilling before he spends it.'

'I don't know, Mr Jobbry; but seats in the House of Commons are seats now: – I mean, the stalls in Smithfield are every year more valuable.'

'Well, Mr Probe, I can make you an offer for my friend, taking the risk of pleasing him upon myself: I can give, I mean for him, a thousand pounds; hear what your client says, and let me know the result: I would say guineas – for I really count on guineas; I wish, however, to have the fifty pounds for a margin – you understand.'

Such was the first consultation, and, considering that I was but a greenhorn in parliamenting, I certainly made an impression.

CHAPTER IV

When Mr Probe had departed, I had a rumination with myself on what had passed, and I could not but think of his expression, 'my client'. It was very clear to me that Mr Curry was the gentleman himself, and therefore I resolved to be on my guard towards him, and to take care not to let him know my suspicion: I also thought, it was very probable, if he were the client spoken of, that he would let his man of business know that I was the true Simon Pure; all which put me on my mettle; and thus it happened, that when he called in the morning, I was prepared; indeed, his calling was to me as a proof from Holy Writ that he was the man himself, for he had no particular occasion to call, nor were we on a footing of such intimacy as to make the civility at all necessary.

But Mr Curry was a pawkie man, and had a reason ready; for he said,

'I just met in the street, as I was coming along, with Mr Probe, and he told me that he had been with you last night.'

'He was,' replied I, 'and seems to be a civil and purpose-like character; but I doubt, Mr Curry, if his client and my friend, you understand, will be able to close.'

'Indeed! why so?'

'Because he expects a greater price than I have made up my mind to give.'

'Oh, there may be some modification. He told me that you had offered only a thousand pounds per session: now, Mr Jobbry, that is rather too little; but you will hear from him what his client says.'

I saw by this that there was a desire on the part of Mr Curry to let me have the seat for what he called a fair price; but having some knowledge of his repute as a man of business, I said briskly, 'I believe, Mr Curry, after all, that this is a very foolish notion of mine. What have I to do with Parliament? it's just an idle longing – the green sickness of idleness. Really, my conversation with Mr Probe has changed my mind in a material degree. What am I to get for a thousand pounds, but two or three franks for letters, and be under an obligation to hear as much nonsense talked across a drinkless table, in the small hours of the night, as ever honest man heard over a jolly bowl? Besides, Mr Curry, if I am to pay money, I have got an inkling that a much better bargain may be had elsewhere.'

I saw that Mr Curry was inoculated with the apprehensions when I said this, for he looked bamboozled; so I followed up the blow with another masterly stroke, adding: 'Indeed, Mr Curry, it would be very foolish extravagance for me to give any such sum as a thousand pounds per session for the vain bauble of a seat; and when ye consider that a whole Parliament can be got, as ye said yourself, for about five thousand pounds, divide that by seven sessions, and ye'll then come nearer what the mark should be.'

'There may be some truth in that, Mr Jobbry,' was the reply; 'but I understood from Mr Probe that you had offered a thousand pounds.'

'Oh! that was in words of course.'

'In parliamentary affairs,' said he, very seriously, 'the strictest honour is to be observed.'

'No doubt; but an agent, you know, cannot pledge himself for his principal, – all is subject to approbation.'

'Yes; but, Mr Jobbry, you are yourself the principal.'

'In a sense, I'll never deny that to you; but Mr Probe only knows me as the friend of a gentleman who has a turn for public speaking, which I have not, and who may turn a penny out of his talent: in short, Mr Curry, something between five hundred and seven hundred is more like a rational price, – I'll give no more.'

'But you have made an offer, sir.'

'Oh! that was in a preliminary way.'

'Mr Probe, however, may insist upon the offer being fulfilled.'

'You must not speak that way to me, or maybe I may, by petition, accuse him to the Honourable House of trafficking in seats, and call you by name as a witness. What would either he or his client say to that?'

I saw that he changed colour, and that his nether lip quivered; so I said to him,

'Between ourselves, Mr Curry, I cannot see the use of shilly-shallying about this, – I'll only give five hundred guineas per session, which, you will allow, is very liberal for a man of honour, who has it in his power, if not well used, to make his complaint to the House.'

'I can only say, Mr Jobbry, that from all I know of the subject, Mr Probe's client will never accept your offer.'

'Very well, that's in his option; but I have an option likewise.'

'What is that?'

'Didn't I hint about petitioning?'

'Mr Jobbry, such a proceeding would be most unparliamentary.'

'No, no, my friend, – don't let us put our heads in the grass, like the foolish ostriches, and think, because we do so, that our hinder ends are not seen: the matter in hand is contrary to law, and therefore we must not apply the rules of law to any thing so nefarious; howsomever, I'll give the five hundred guineas, as I have said.'

'You will never get the seat for that.'

'That may be true; but the Honourable House, like a Spartan judge, is desperate in punishing a detected delinquent: in short, Mr Curry, if ye have anything to say anent this negotiation, ye'll advise a compliance with my proposition.'

I could discern that Mr Curry was in a frying condition; but he was a man of experience, and it was not in my power to draw out of him that he was at all art or part in the business; so, not to waste time with more talk, I passed into the news of the day, and Mr Curry presently took his leave; while I very much wondered at my own instinct in acquiring the art of parliamenting so readily; and I had soon good cause, as I shall presently shew, for the address with which I was on that occasion gifted.

CHAPTER V

There was something which struck me in that conversation with Mr Curry not altogether conciliatory; and after pondering over it for some time, I came to a conclusion that presently Mr Probe would come to me with a new offer. I thereupon resolved to bide in the coffee-house all day, that I might not be wanting in the needful season. The day, no doubt, was no temptation, inasmuch as it was rainy, and the streets in a very slobbery condition, and I had no particular business to call me abroad. Accordingly, it fell out just as I expected. About the heel of the evening, the waiter came to see what I would have for dinner, and said to me, in a kind of parenthesis, as I was looking over the bill of fare, that he supposed I should not want the private room that evening.

'My lad,' quo' I, 'that's very correct of you, for I had forgot that maybe the same gentleman who was with me yesterday may call again; I therefore think it will be just as commodious to have my dinner laid in the parlour as in this, the coffee-room; so you'll just attend to that.'

'Very well,' said he, and did as I desired; and well it was for me that he had been so considerate, for, before the dinner was ready, who should come in but Mr Probe; and after various hithers and yons, I invited him to dine with me, the night being very wet; to the which, after some entreaty, he was consenting, and thereupon we went up into the private room, and had a couple of candles and our dinner duly served.

For some time, and especially while we were eating, I thought that it was judicious to say nothing to him concerning the manor of Humbug; but when we were satisfied, the cloth withdrawn, and Carbonell again upon the table, we opened the debate.

'Mr Probe,' said I, 'since I had the felicity of conversing with you concerning that weak plan of my friend's about going into Parliament, – for weak I say it is, as I see no whereby he can make profit of his outlay, – I have thought I cannot better do a friend's part than advise him to have nothing to do with such an inconvenience.'

'My good Mr Jobbry,' said he, 'no one can dispute your prudence in that matter; for no man in his senses, I mean in his sober senses, would ever think of spending his nights in hearing young men, of a very moderate capacity, talking by the hour; but that is not our present purpose: my business is, as they say in the House, to report progress; and what I have to mention is, that I have seen my client and communicated your offer.'

'My offer, Mr Probe? what do you mean? surely you could never consider our few preliminary words as a serious overture?'

'Mr Jobbry,' replied the ruddy little man, 'did not you tell me that you would give a thousand pounds per session for I'll not say what?'

'Most certainly I did, Mr Probe; most certainly I gave it as my opinion that a thousand pounds was quite enough; but there is a wide difference between giving an opinion on the value of a thing, and buying that thing. Now, I was clearly made up in my mind that a thousand pounds was the full value of your client's sitting part; but the worth to my friend was another question.'

'Mr Jobbry, I considered we had done some business together; you made an offer – I reported that offer – and you have your answer.'

'Very right, Mr Probe, you speak like a man of business; I like to deal with off-hand people – there is nothing like frankness; but if you thought that I made a definitive offer, you were never more mistaken in your life.'

'You don't say so? – this is very awkward.'

'Oh, not at all, not at all; we were only talking upon the general question; and I think, Mr Probe, considering it as an opening conversation, we advanced pretty well to the point: but you must know, sir, that I could not bind my principal without his own consent.'

At these words, I observed Mr Probe looking at me with a kind of left-handed peering, which left no doubt in my mind that Mr Curry had reported progress too, and asked leave to sit again; but I was on my guard.

'I shall not controvert that, Mr Jobbry,' said Mr Probe, 'but the mistake has been committed, certainly.'

'If you think so, Mr Probe, I shall very much regret it on your account; but with me, in my usual way, all was plain sailing, – and if you will ask our mutual friend, Mr Curry, who was here with me in the morning, he will tell you that I told him five hundred guineas was the full and adequate price of the article.'

'This is surprising! To what purpose did we speak, if you did not authorise me to offer a thousand pounds?'

'Mr Probe, I am a greenhorn, and not versed in the diplomaticals; but it was not reasonable to come upon me in that way, without even

17

knowing the name of the borough, and who were to be my constituents. That simple fact, Mr Probe, shews you have been greatly mistaken in supposing my words of course contained a specific offer.'

'Well, let that pass; all I had to say was, that my client was not indisposed to listen to your offer.'

'Now, Mr Probe,' said I, 'don't your own words confirm what I was saying? If I had made an offer, would not your client have given an answer either in the affirmative or in the negative? And yet you say that he was only not indisposed to listen to my proposal.'

'Well, well,' said Mr Probe, 'you attach a little more importance to the accidental word "indisposed" than I intended; and therefore you will excuse me if I request you to say in few words what you will give, that there may be no mistake this time.'

'My principal,' said I, 'is a prudent man.'

'So I perceive,' said Mr Probe.

And I added that, 'I had told Mr Curry I thought, and did think, five hundred guineas a liberal price.'

'I shall report that,' said Mr Probe; 'but it is too little.'

'Then, if you think so, let the business end. I am very indifferent about the subject; and, besides, I have good reason to think that, under particular circumstances, seats can be had cheaper, Mr Probe.'

'My object, Mr Jobbry, in being with you is to do business: it is nothing to me what you know or what you offer; I am but an agent.'

'I see that,' replied I; 'you are the go-between.'

'Well, well, that office must be done by somebody; let us make a minute of agreement for seven hundred pounds.'

'No, no; five hundred guineas is the ultimate.'

'You are a strange gentleman,' said he. 'Make it six hundred guineas, to end the matter.'

'No,' said I; 'no guineas above the five hundred: but I'll make it pounds, which you will agree is very extravagant.'

Thus, from less to more, we came to an agreement, and signed mutual missives to that effect; and a pawkie laugh we had together, as well as a fresh bottle of Carbonell's, when it came out that Mr Curry was 'my client', as I had jaloused; and that I was to succeed him as the honourable member for Frailtown, when he had taken the Chiltern Hundreds.

CHAPTER VI

Having thus explained my popular election for the well-known ancient borough of Frailtown, as the member for which I made my appearance among the knights and burgesses in Parliament assembled, I will now proceed to relate what next came to pass.

It will be seen that I took my seat in the middle of the session, which many of my Indian friends thought was a souple trick, because the event at the time made no noise; whereas, if I had waited for the general election, that ill-tongued tinkler, the daily press, would have been pouking at my tail maybe, as I was going in, duly elected, among the rest of the clanjamfrey.

No sooner had I, as it was stated in the newspapers, taken the oaths and my seat, than I lifted my eyes and looked about me; and the first and foremost resolution that I came to, was, not to take a part at first in the debates. I was above the vain pretension of making speeches; I knew that a wholesome member of Parliament was not talkative, but attended to solid business; I was also convinced, that unless I put a good price on my commodity, there would be no disposition to deal fairly by me. Accordingly, I resolved for the first week not to take my seat in any particular part of the House, but to shift from side to side with the speakers on the question, as if to hear them better; and this I managed in so discreet a manner, that I observed by the Friday night, when there was a great splore, that the ministers, from the treasury bench, pursued me with their eyes to fascinate me, wondering, no doubt, with what side I would vote, – but I voted with neither. That same evening, more than two of my friends inquired of me what I thought of the question. By this I could guess that my conduct was a matter of speculation; so I said to them that, 'really, much was to be said on both sides; but I had made up my mind not to vote the one way or the other until I got a convincing reason.'

This was thought a good joke, and so it was circulated through the House, inasmuch as that, when we broke up at seven o'clock on the Saturday morning, one of the ministers, a young soft-headed lad, took hold of me by the arm, in the lobby, and inquired, in a jocund manner, if I had got a convincing reason. I gave him thereupon a nod and a

19

wink, and said, "Not yet; but I expected one soon, when I would do myself the honour of calling upon him'; which he was very well pleased to hear, and shook me by the hand with a cordiality by common when he wished me good night, – 'trusting,' as he said, 'that we should soon be better acquainted.' 'It will not be my fault,' quo' I, 'if we are not.'

With that we parted; and I could see by the eye in my neck that he thought, with the light head of youth, that he had made a capital conquest, by his condescension.

Now, this small matter requires an explanation, for the benefit of other new members. If a man has all his eyes about him, he will soon discern that a ministry, if it has three or four decent, auld-farrent men, is for the most part composed of juveniles – state 'prentices – the sprouts and offshoots of the powerful families. With them lies the means of conciliating members; for the weightier metal of the ministers is employed in public affairs, and to the younkers is confided the distribution of the patronage, – for a good reason, it enables them to make friends and a party by the time that they come, in the course of nature, to inherit the upper offices.

I had not been long in the House till I noticed this; and as my object in being at the expense of going thereinto was to make power for myself, I was not displeased at the scion of nobility making up to me; and I have uniformly since found, that the true way of having a becoming influence with government, is slily to get the upper hand of the state fry.

But, on this occasion, there was a personal reason for my so cleverly saying I would call on him for a convincing reason. My second cousin, James Gled, when he saw my election in the newspapers, wrote to me for my interest, knowing that I would naturally be on the side of Government, and stating that the office of distributor of stamps in our county was soon to be vacant. So it just came into my head in the nick of time to make a pleasant rejoinder to my lord; and accordingly I was as good as my word; and to make the matter as easy as possible, I told him, in my jocular manner, when I called, that I was come for the convincing reason.

I could see that he was a little more starched in his office than in the lobby; but I was determined to be troubled with no diffidence, and said, 'My lord, you'll find me a man open to conviction – a very small reason will satisfy me at this time; but, to be plain with your lordship, I must have a reason, – not that I say the Government is far wrong, but

20

I have an inclination to think that the Opposition is almost in the right.'
And then I stated to his lordship, in a genteel manner, what James Gled
had said to me, adding, 'It's but a small place, and maybe your lordship
would think me more discreet if I would lie by for something better;
but I wish to convince his Majesty's Government that I'm a moderate
man, of a loyal inclination.'

His lordship replied, 'That he had every inclination to serve an
independent member, but the King's government could not be carried
on without patronage; he was, however, well disposed to oblige me.'

'My lord,' said I, 'if I was seeking a favour for myself, I would not
ask for such a paltry place as this; but I'm a man that wants nothing:
only it would be a sort of satisfaction to oblige this very meritorious
man, Mr Gled.'

We had then some further talk; and he gave me a promise, that if
the place was not given away, my friend should have it.

'I'm very much obliged to you, my lord, for this earnest of your
good-will to me; and really, my lord, had I thought you were so well
inclined, I would have looked for a more convincing reason': at which
he laughed, and so we parted. But, two days after, when the vacancy
was declared, he said to me, with a sly go, 'That I was a man very hard
to be convinced, and required a powerful argument.'

'My lord,' quo' I, 'I did not hope to be taunted in this manner for
applying to your lordship to serve an honest man with such a bit
trifling post.'

'Trifling?' he exclaimed; 'it is a thousand a-year at least!'

'Well, my lord, if it be, Mr Gled is as well worthy of it as another;
I want nothing myself; but if your lordship thinks that the Government
is to be served by over-valuing small favours, my course in Parliament
is very clear.'

His lordship upon this was of a lowlier nature than I could have
expected, and therefore I reined myself in to moderation; for I saw I
had gotten an advantage, and in more ways than one. This was the
case; for in my Indian ignorance I thought a distributor of stamps was
some beggarly concern of a hundred a-year, but a thousand was really
past hope; it was, however, not judicious to think so before my lord.

CHAPTER VII

When I came to consider that the place I had gotten for my relation James Gled was so very lucrative, I really felt as if I had committed a mistake, and was very angry with myself; but in reflecting a little more upon the subject, I saw that it might be turned to great public good: for inasmuch as the places and posts of Government belong to those members and others that get nothing else for their services in support of Government, a judicious man will husband his share of them, so as to make the distribution go as far as possible. Accordingly, as I well knew that two hundred and fifty pounds a-year would have been a most liberal godsend to James, I thought that if it were three it would be a great thing, and that there would be seven hundred over, to apply to other public purposes. I thereupon wrote to him, and said that I had got the place for him, but that his salary was to be three hundred a-year, the remainder being subject to another disposal.

In due course of post I received a most thankful letter for my beneficence, agreeing most willingly to be content with his share of the allowed emoluments. When I got this letter, and got James established in his place, I then bethought me of the most judicious appropriation that could be made of the surplus; and there anent I called to mind a son that I had in the natural way, who was in the army. To him I portioned out three hundred pounds per annum, for he had been a very heavy cess on me, notwithstanding he was serving his king and country; and this, it will be allowed, was as correct a doing as any arrangement of the kind; far more so than that of those who have large pensions themselves, from which they make allowances to their sons, although these sons be of the patriots that make speeches to mobs and multitudes, declaring themselves as pure men, unsullied by any ailment drawn from the people; which is, in a sense, no doubt, the fact, for their allowances are from their fathers.

Having given the three hundred to Captain Jobbry, I then thought of old Mrs Hayning, my aunt, who was the widow of the minister of Dargorble, and had nothing but her widow's fund to live upon. So I gave her one hundred pounds, which, it will be allowed, was to her a great thing, and it was a very just thing; for as the clergy have no right to make money of their stipends, if they keep up their station and act charitably, the nation should provide for their widows. The remaining three hundred I stipulated with James Gled should be laid aside in the bank, year by year, to be a fund from which I should, from time to time, contribute to public subscriptions; and few things in my life have I been more satisfied with: for so long as James Gled lived, it will be seen by the newspapers what a liberal subscriber I was thereby enabled to be to public charities, by which I acquired great rule and power in them; and many a poor man's child, and orphan likewise, have I been the means of getting well educated. Indeed, I take some blame to myself that I did not more rigidly enforce the same principle of distribution in the salaries of all the posts that I got, at different times, for my kindred and constituents.

There is, however, no condition of life without a drawback on its satisfactions; and of this truth I had soon due experience. From time to time it had been a custom with the member for Frailtown, when he happened to be of ministerial principles, to give a bit small postie to some well-recommended inhabitant of the borough; and accordingly, some anxiety was always taken to ascertain that their new member was a man of the convenient sort. Thus it came to pass, that I had not well warmed my seat when Mr Spicer, a shopkeeper, and a member of the corporation, called on me one morning and introduced himself; for, as I had never been at Frailtown, I was, of course, in dead ignorance of all my constituents; but when he had made himself known, I received him in a very civilised manner, and inquired in what way I could serve the borough.

Thereupon we had a conversation concerning a canal that was to pass at some short distance from Frailtown; and Mr Spicer shewed me a very great advantage that it would be of, could ways and means be raised, to make a cut into the town; plainly, as I could see, thinking that, if I did not do it at my own cost, I might, by a liberal contribution, be helping thereunto.

This I thought, at the time, in my own heart, was a very barefaced hope of the corporation to entertain; for I had paid the full price of my seat. But as I had ends to serve with the borough, as well as the corporation thought it had ends to serve with me, I replied to Mr Spicer, in a very debonair manner:

'Mr Spicer,' quo' I, 'it really gives me great pleasure to hear that you, in that part of England, are in such a very thriving condition; by the by, in what county is Frailtown?'

When he had made answer that it was in Vamptonshire, I said, 'That I had no notion it was such a prospering district; and that surely I would do all in my power, as a Member of Parliament, to further any bill for the benefit of a community with which I was so nearly and dearly connected': adding, 'It was, however, with me a rule never to contribute to the improvement of any other property than my own, especially as I was at that time laying out a great sum in repairs upon my house, in addition to the improvements on my estate. But,' continued I, 'you are free to use my name as patronising the undertaking.'

'Well,' said he, 'that's, no doubt, something; but though it may not be commodious to you to advance money, I have thought – considering your great influence with the Government – that some time or another you may have it in your power to befriend an honest man.'

'Nothing,' said I, 'would give me greater pleasure: what sort of a post are you looking to?' I added, laughing: 'something, no doubt, more lucrative than the gallows?'

'Oh, me! I am looking for none, thank Heaven; I am content with my own business for the present; but I have a daughter married to a most deserving young man, who would be right glad to be made post-master in the village of Physickspring, which is within two miles of our town, and which gets its letters by an old man from our office.'

'I should think, Mr Spicer, such a place would not be worth the asking for.'

'Nor would it,' said he, 'but Physickspring is growing a watering-place, and it is for futurity that he will accept it.'

'But does your son-in-law live there, that he would take such a place?'

'Not yet, Mr Jobbry; but he intends to take up a shop of perfumes and nick-knackeries, jewellery, and other gaieties; and he thinks it would help to bring custom to his shop, if he could conjoin the business thereunto of post-master.'

This seemed a very rational proposition; though I could not help laughing in my sleeve to hear that the honest man believed, in seeking to help a friend, I did not see he was really helping himself; – but we are short-sighted creatures, and such self-delusion is not uncommon.

However, to oblige Mr Spicer, I promised to exert my best capability to serve his friend; and as the thing was but a trifle, I soon secured it for him; although I learned with surprise that there were no less than five other applicants.

'Oh, ho!' thought I, when I heard this, 'it cannot be such a trifling place.' However, as little was known concerning it, I said nothing, but got the appointment for Mr Spicer's son-in-law. The five applications, however, stuck in my throat; and before communicating to him the appointment, I thought it was a duty incumbent to make some inquiry; and accordingly I did so, as I shall shew forth in the next chapter.

CHAPTER VIII

I found, on inquiry, that Frailtown was a decayed place, and that Physickspring was fast flourishing in repute – that in a few years it had outnumbered Frailtown by a great deal – and that from the time the Duchess of Driveabout had made it her place of resort, the visitors were most genteel and select; insomuch, that for one letter that went to Frailtown, a score at least went to Physickspring. This assured me that the separate post-office that was to be established would beat the old one all to shivers. I likewise learned, that the post-office in Frailtown had been long kept by the widow of a former mayor, who had brought up a decent family of daughters in the church of England and the Christian religion; and that since the increase of Physickspring they were well to do in the world, being milliners. It was therefore very plain to me, that the new establishment would not only be a great drawback on them, but a total loss to old Edward Dawner, the man that distributed the letters in Physickspring.

This, it will be seen, was a case that required prudent handling; and I resolved to weigh the whole circumstances thereof in a judicious balance. At first, my natural inclination was to advise the milliners to move their business to Physickspring, and to keep old Edward Dawner as the postman to go with the letters to Frailtown; in fact, just to reverse the practice. I heard, however, that the Misses Stiches had the whole business of Frailtown, which they would lose if they removed to Physickspring, where they had no chance of success, as a fashionable nymph of the gumflowers, from London, had forestalled the trade. Indeed, I saw that when a man obtains a share in the distributions of the good things of Government, it behoves him not to allow himself to be overly yielding to his natural tender feelings; and thus I was constrained, by a public duty, to make the best arrangement I could in the difficulties of the case; and what I did, got me great respect over all that country side. I got an inkling from the post-office concerning the value of the postmastership of Frailtown, the which I saw was very handsome in moderation. I therefore wrote to Mr Spicer, that I had got a conditional grant of the office for his son-in-law, but which I was afraid made it so little worth, that he would not think of accepting the same – that the conditions were to the effect that one Edward Dawner was to be indemnified by an annual sum of money, whenever the postmaster's allowance exceeded thirty pounds a-year – I had ascertained that it was well on to four times that amount; and that Mrs Stiches was likewise to have an indemnity, and should be paid, whenever the emoluments exceeded fifty pounds a-year clear, all surplus till she had five-and-twenty pounds a-year.

After stating these particulars to Mr Spicer, I said to him, in my letter, that he would tell his son-in-law what I would do for him, provided that the place, with such burdens, was an object.

As I expected, back in course of post came a letter accepting the offer, but in a cool way. The arrangement, however, was greatly applauded by the inhabitants of the borough, as well as by the gentry at Physickspring, and every one there said it consisted with reason that there should be a post-office at such a growing place; and that it shewed I was a man of reflection and observation to put such a judicious idea into the head of Government. In short, I was a very popular member; and I must say, though I say it myself, deservedly so. 'Deal small, and serve all,' was an ancient proverb that I gave great heed to; and the first session of my parliamentary career shews that I understood its application.

So much anent the second administration of my influence in my first session, when I was in a manner innocent of the ways and means of dealing with patronage. As I became better acquainted with the usages of Parliament, no doubt I grew more dexterous; but on no future occasion did I ever make such a sensible appropriation as on those just mentioned, which I partly attribute to my being a fresh hand in the business – 'new brooms', as the saying is, 'sweep clean'; and I was then spank new in ministerious trafficking: indeed, I had then more leisure, and had time to consider what I was about; but afterwards, as will be shewn by and by, when I came to have my hands full of committee-work, private bills, and local affairs, I could afford less time to attend to the distribution of the salaries in the manner I have described; and here it becomes me to make a very cogent remark.

In those days there had been none of that heresy about savings, which has been such a plague both to ministers and members of late years. We then all sat each under his vine and fig-tree; and there was then really some enjoyment in making the people happy, especially those who had for friends members that were of the salutary way of thinking. I am, however, anticipating much of what I have to relate, and the sore changes that have come to pass among us since that fatal night when a late member betrayed us, by calling our right to share in the patronage by the ignominious epithet of candle-ends and cheese-parings; for, ever since, it has been thought that we have been wanting to our own wisdom, in being so inveterate to retain the distribution of places and pensions – the natural perquisites of Members of Parliament.

CHAPTER IX

My first session in Parliament was a time of bustle; as much, however, owing to my being still a novice in the business, as to the concerns in which I took an interest: but I gradually quieted down into more method; and, as practice makes perfect, before the session was concluded, I began to know, in a measure, what I was about, and could see that some change of a molesting kind was impending over us.

The French revolution had done a deal of damage to all those establishments which time and law had taken so much pains to construct; but nothing which it caused was so detrimental to the stability of things, as the introduction of that evil notion among mankind, that the people were the judges of the posts and perquisites about Government; for although it is very true that the means of paying for these things is drawn from the nation at large, it is not very clear that there is any class of the people competent to judge of the whole subject. It is surely consistent with nature that governments should be made out of the first people for rank, talent, and property, in the kingdom, and that they should have allowances and privileges, under regulation, suitable to their high stations. Now, how can the lower orders and the commonalty be judges of what is a fit recompense for persons of the degree alluded to? Operatives would think a very small salary a great deal, as compared with their earnings; and, no doubt, the higher orders are equally unjust when they attempt to value the remuneration of labour. The democratical, for example, think state salaries always exorbitant, and the aristocratical never think wages low enough: out of this controversy between them has arisen many of those troubles which eyes that are not yet opened will be closed by old age and death before they are ended; for it is now no longer possible to prevent the world from conceiving itself qualified to judge of what a nation should pay to its servants. Every man, now-a-days, thinks he has a right to tell what the nation shall pay, and yet conceits that no one has a right to interfere with him. Surely it is not consistent with common sense, that the mobility, who talk so much about the corruption of places and pensions, should be the judges of the recompense that is due for the services of men of high degree; and yet it is this which is the cause of our vexations. No doubt, it is very wrong that any class, faction, or party, in the state, should monopolise the patronage of the whole state: but there is a wide difference between *that*, which some say renders reform needful, and that pretence to regulate the emoluments and salaries of the state by the public voice. Salaries are great or small relative to their duties and stations. The chiefs of the state must keep up an equality of station with those of the highest rank in the kingdom; and those of every degree under them must maintain a like equality with the class of persons that their public duties require them to act and associate with: it is therefore, in my opinion, a most heterodox way of thinking, to imagine that the private property of individuals of high rank is to remain untouched, and yet that the officers of state, who must necessarily be their associates and companions, shall be reduced to comparative poverty. I am the more particular in explaining my view on this subject, because, in common with other honourable members, I have felt, as will be in due time shewn, very serious annoyance from the new-fangled doctrines of the Utilitarians. And here, before I proceed with my narrative, I may as well observe, that there is, in my opinion, a great fallacy about this new-light doctrine of utility, as something distinct from happiness. I consider, and it has been so considered from the beginning of the world, that the object of all utility is happiness; but every man's happiness does not lie in the same circumstances, and therefore there can be no universal method of producing happiness by utility. No doubt it is useful to get public affairs administered as cheaply as possible; but if the chiefs of the state must be the companions of the high and rich, you will never get men of talent to fill these offices, without exposing them to the hazard of committing high crimes and misdemeanours, to procure indirectly the wherewithal to keep up their equality.

Having thus stated my ideas upon the rightfulness of regulating salaries of public officers by the way of living among those with whom their public duties require them to associate, it will be seen that I have, in always voting with the ministers against the reduction of salaries, only acted on the soundest principles; for even in the matter of sinecures, I have adhered with constancy to my principles. Sinecures ought not to be considered as salaries for doing nothing, but as salaries set apart nominally for the use of those dependants of influential people whom it is necessary to conciliate to the Government. All governments must have various means of conciliating various men: there must be titles and degrees for those whom such baubles please; there must be

30

enterprises and commands for those who delight in adventures; and there must be sinecures and pensions for the sordid. It is as much to be lamented that such humours are entailed upon our common nature, as it is to be mourned that it is liable to so many various diseases; but it is an ignorant mistake of the nature of man to think the world is to be ruled by one class of motives.

Such were the reflections which occupied my mind during the recess of Parliament after my first session. I was thankful that my fortune enabled me to be independent, and that I had no natural turn for the diplomatics of politics; but I learned, from conversing with politicians, something of the state at which society was arrived, and saw the necessity of having clear ideas regarding those matters in which I was most interested; for my object in going into Parliament was to help my kith and kin by a judicious assistance to Government, and it was of great importance that the assistance should be given on a conscientious principle. Accordingly, by these reflections I was persuaded, that, from the state of the times and public opinion, no member of the House should, without the clearest views as well as convincing reasons, consent to the creation of new places, nor, be it observed also, to the abolition of old places; and this led me to a very manifest conclusion.

It appeared, when I came to think of it, that the great cause which stirred men to be in opposition to Government was to provide for their friends and dependants, and that that was the secret reason why the Opposition found such fault with existing institutions and places, and why they put forth new plans of national improvement, which they pledged themselves, if ever they got into office, to carry into effect. Time has verified this notion. Under the pretext of instituting better official and judicature arrangements, new ones have been introduced by the Opposition when they came into power, which enabled them to provide for their friends and dependants; but they were obliged to indemnify those who enjoyed the old offices. Whether the change was an improvement or not, I would not undertake to maintain; but the alteration was very conducive to the acquisition of a new stock of patronage. With very little individual suffering, the change necessarily superseded and set aside those who did the work under the old system; but as there would have been gross injustice in turning adrift the old servants, they were provided for by an indemnification, and the new servants had all the new places to themselves over and above: in time, as the old servants died off, the evil was remedied.

CHAPTER X

When my second session was about to commence, I went to London several days before the opening of Parliament. In this I was incited by a very laudable desire; for the more I reflected on the nature of my public trusts, the plainer I saw that the obligations on a member were more and more manifold; so I resolved to occupy the few preliminary days in going about among the friends and acquaintances that I had made in the former session, and to consult with them concerning the state of things in general: thus it happened that I was very particular in conferring with old Sir John Bulky.

The baronet was a member for a borough in his own county, and had been so for six successive Parliaments; being a good neighbour, a very equitable magistrate, and in all respects a most worthy country gentleman, upholding the laws and the power of Government around him with courageous resolution in the worst of times. But he was grown old and afflicted with the gout, suffering indeed so often from it, that his attendance in the House was frequently interrupted. I had seen his superior sagacity the preceding year, and sometimes we took tea upstairs together when there was a heavy debate, out of which grew between us a very confidential friendship.

Sir John and I very cordially met. He had during the recess been not quite so well in his health as usual, but he had been free of the gout; and it had happened that his eldest son, who had been abroad to see the world, had come home, and that, in consequence, his house had been filled with company for the summer. Many of the guests were also travelled men; and he had opportunities of hearing from them more concerning the state of the continent, as well as respecting society at home, than usual. We had therefore, at our first meeting, a very solid conversation on public affairs, and were quite in unison in our notion that, although the French revolution had gone past the boiling, it was yet in a state to keep the world long in hot water.

'Depend on it, Mr Jobbry,' said the worthy baronet, 'it will be long before the ruins of the earthquake settle into solid ground; and although Buonaparte and his abettors must be put down for our own sakes, it cannot be denied that the French are well content with him; yet when they are put down, it will be only another revolution. The first came out of themselves upon their neighbours – the next will come from their neighbours upon them; so between the two, at the end of the second revolution I should not wonder if the world were to be found in looser disorder than at the first, which will make the part of Britain the more difficult; for, of all nations in Europe, we are the most apt, by our freedom, to catch the infection of opinions.'

'That's strange, Sir John,' quo' I; 'for inasmuch as we are in a state of advance to the nations of the continent, it's wonderful that we should think their crude dreams and theories objects of imitation for us to follow, which indeed we cannot do unless we go backward.'

'It is, Mr Jobbry, however, the case. I have lived long enough in public to observe that every season has its own peculiar malady both moral and physical, and that it rarely happens that men continue in the same mind on public questions for two years together; in short, that the art of keeping the world steady, and which is the art of government, is to find the ways and means to amuse mankind. It is, no doubt, true that the disease of every year is not attended with such high delirium as we have seen of late; but still there is always that morbid disposition about nations that requires great delicacy in the management; and experience has taught me to have a great distrust of general reformations; indeed, it seems to be the course of Providence to make the most fatal things ever appear the fairest; and I never hear of the alluring plausibilities of changes in the state of the world, without having an apprehension that these changes, which promise so much good, are the means by which Providence is working an overthrow.'

When we had discoursed in this manner for some time, he then told me that he had heard it said the Government was going to reduce all things that could be well spared.

'In a sense, Sir John,' said I, 'nothing can be more plausible; but they cannot reduce the establishments without making so many people poorer and obliging them to reduce their establishments, thereby spreading distress and privation wider. It is not a time to reduce public appointments when there is national distress; the proper season is when all is green and flourishing.'

'Very true,' replied Sir John; 'it would seem that the best time of providing for those who must be discharged when governments reduce their appointments, is when new employments are easy to be had; but things at present look not very comfortable in that way, and therefore

I am grieved to hear that the distemper of making saving to the general state at the expense of casting individuals into poverty, has infected the Government. In truth, Mr Jobbry, this intelligence has distressed me quite as much as a change of administration would; for a change of administration does not make actual distress, inasmuch as the new ministers always create, in redeeming their pledges, a certain number of new places, and commonly indemnify for those they abolish; but a mere system of economising – of lessening expenditure during a period of general hardship – is paving the way to revolution; and accordingly, as I am too old now to take a part in so busy a scene, I intend to retire at the close of the present Parliament.'

'And,' quo' I, 'have you arranged yet for your successor in Easyborough?'

'Not yet,' said he; 'for, to tell you the truth, that's the chief object that has brought me to town. I have sat for six Parliaments for the borough, and it has never cost me any thing; and I know that whoever I recommend will be received with a strong feeling of good-will, which makes me a little chary on the subject; for I would not like to recommend to them a man that was not deserving of their confidence.'

'That's very creditable to you, Sir John; but I should think that they would be right willing to accept your son.'

'True, Mr Jobbry, I have no doubt they would accept very willingly my son; but I am not sure that he is just the man fit for them; for though he is a young man of good parts, he has got too many philosophical crotchets about the rules and principles of government, to be what in my old-fashioned notions I think a useful English legislator. He's honest and he's firm, but honesty and firmness are not enough; there is a kind of consideration that folly is entitled to, that honesty and firmness will not grant. I don't know, Mr Jobbry, if I make you understand me; but as the object of all political power is to make people happy, the right sort of member for Easyborough is a person well advanced in life, and of more good-nature in his humours than rigid righteousness in his principles. My son would do better, and would be a good member for a patriotic community; but the orderly and soberminded inhabitants of Easyborough require a man of a different character.'

'And have you found nobody yet, Sir John, that you would recommend?'

'No,' says he, 'no.'

'I wish,' quo' I, 'that you would think well of me; for I would fain make an exchange for Frailtown; could not you let your son and me make an arrangement for an exchange?'

'No,' said Sir John; 'because I could not recommend you to Easy-borough.'

I felt the blood rush into my face at this very plain dealing; and, just to be as plain, said,

'What's your objection, Sir John?'

'Nothing to you as a man, Mr Jobbry, for I think you both shrewd and clever; but because you have not yet got right notions of what belongs to the public; you take too close and personal an interest for your own sake in your borough. Now that does not consort with my notions – my constituents have never cost me a guinea, and they have never asked me for a favour – a constituency of that kind would not suit you, Mr Jobbry.'

Soon after this point of conversation, I bade him good morning, and came away; but what he said made a deep impression, and I was really displeased at his opinion of me, which led me to adopt the resolutions and line of conduct that will be described in the next chapter. But the House of Commons, it is well known, is a school of ill manners; and a long sederunt as a member does not tend to mitigate plain speaking.

CHAPTER XI

A man who observes sharply, as I have been in the practice of doing all my reasonable life, will not be long in Parliament till he has full occupation for his faculties. It is a place not just like the world, but is, in fact, a community made up of a peculiar people, and the members are more unlike to one another than the generality of mankind, and have upon them, besides, a stamp and impress of character that makes them as visibly a distinct race in the world, as the marking of sheep distinguishes one flock from another at tryst or market.

This diversity, in my opinion, proceeds from two causes; the one is, that every thing a member says in the House is received as truth; and thus it happens when an orator is under an obligation, either from friendship or party spirit, to blink the veracity of his subject, he is put to a necessity of using roundabout words, that feed the ear and yet cheat the mind in the sense; and this begets a formality of language that really makes some Members of Parliament very quiscus and unsatisfactory to have business to do with. The other cause comes from the reverse of this, inasmuch as there is no restraint but a man's own discretion, in what he states; and as all men are not alike gifted with that blessing, a Parliament fool is far more remarkable than a weak man out of doors; and thus it is, that honourable members have, in addition to their worldly character, a parliamentary character; but some put on the parliamentary character, not having those habits by which it is induced; and these, to any observant man, are really very amusing and ridiculous: they are, for the most part, the silent voters on both sides of the House; chiefly, however, of the Government thick-and-thinners.

When I had, to my perfect satisfaction, ascertained the accuracy of this opinion, I came to a resolution that begat me in time a very sedate and respectable reputation. Several times, during my first session, I had a mind to speak; and, really, there were speeches spoken which were most instigating to me to hear, and provoking me to reply; but, somehow, my heart failed, and the session passed over without my getting up. This at the time was not very satisfactory to myself, and I daresay if the session had continued a little longer, I might have been so bold as to utter a few words: but during the recess I had a consultation with myself relative to my habits and abilities; and I came in consequence to a resolution, that, as I was not sure of possessing the talent of eloquence, never having tried it, I should not, without a necessity, make the endeavour, – a resolution which I have had great reason to rejoice in, because, in the second session, various questions were debated, that, if I had possessed a disposition to speak, I would have expressed myself in a manner that might not have been applauded by the public. My silence, therefore, enabled me to escape animadversion; and I was protected also from acquiring any of that parliamentary character, as to the choice of terms, to which I have been alluding. Thank Heaven! I have had gumption enough left to avoid assuming it; for verily it is a droll thing to hear men that are everlasting silent ciphers in the House, speaking (when you meet with them at dinner) across the table as if they were the very ora rotundas of the Treasury bench.

I had another advantage in resolving to be only a vote – and that was, it committed me upon but few questions; by which I was left free to do as I pleased with ministers, in case a change should take place between the two sides of the House. In all the regular business of Government, my loyalty and principles led me to uphold the public service; but on those occasions when the outs and ins amused themselves with a field-day, or a benefit-night rather, I very often did not vote at all, – for I never considered pairing off before the division as fully of the nature of a vote; and several times, when the minister who had the management of the House spoke to me for going away before the debate was done, I explained to him why I did so, by saying that I always went off when I saw that the Government party had the best of the argument, and thought that maybe if I had staid till the back of the bow-wows against them were up, I might be seduced from my allegiance, and constrained by their speeches to give a vote according to my conscience, as it might be moulded by their oratory.

I will not say, in a very positive manner, that all the members who pair off during the middle of a debate are actuated by the principle of fairness that I was; but some, no doubt, are; for it's really a hard thing for a man to be convinced by a speech from the Opposition, and yet be obliged, by the principle that attaches him to the Government, to give a vote against his conscience. In short, by the time that the second session was half over, I had managed myself with such a canny sobriety, that my conduct was regarded with very considerable deference. I was a most attentive member, whether in my attendance on committees

37

or in the House; and I carried my particularity to so exact a degree, that even in the number of my daily franks I allowed myself to incur not the loss of one; and I was so severe in the administration of even this small privilege, that I never borrowed a frank from a friend.

It may seem that my correctness in this matter of the franks was a trifle not worth mentioning; but I had my own ends for it. It was the last session of a Parliament; and it is very curious what an insight it afforded me of the puetering that some men that had boroughs to contest carried on; for whenever I saw a friend writing often, and needing many franks to the same borough, I concluded that he had an election purpose to accomplish.

Towards the end of the session, I observed that a young man, Mr Gabblon, was very industrious, almost every day getting franks; and although I was regular in the smoking-room, he never once applied to me. One day, when I was sitting there by myself, and he came in to get a cover additional to his own, – seeing me alone, he went immediately out, without asking my assistance. This I thought very comical; and it immediately flashed like lightning on my mind, that, surely, he could not be undermining my interest in Frailtown?

It is wonderful to think what queer and ingenious thoughts will come into people's heads. No sooner did the surmise rise in my mind, than I was moved by an inordinate impulse to learn if there was anything in his correspondence to justify the suspicion, and I was not long left in doubt; for soon after came in another member, with whom I was on the best of footings; and he had a blank cover in his hand, which he addressed at the table and gave out to Mr Gabblon, who was standing in the lobby. When my friend had done so, I said,

'That young lad, Mr Gabblon, has a wonderful large correspondence. What can he be about? for these several days he has been always in want of franks; and yet he is not a man of commerce, but a squire.'

My friend, Mr Henwick, looked to me very slily, and said, 'did I really not know what Mr Gabblon was about?'

'No; I don't trouble myself with other people's affairs: but it is surprising how men that have no business should have such a correspondence.'

'Well,' said Mr Henwick, 'what you say is extraordinary. Have you not heard that Mr Gabblon intends to succeed you in Frailtown; and his correspondence is with the influential people of your own borough?'

'No possible!' said I.

'But it is true,' said he with a smile; and some of us, seeing you were taking no step, concluded that you intended to retire from Parliament.'

'This is news, Mr Henwick,' replied I, and it behoves me to look after it. I wonder, indeed, what could make him think of cutting me out.'

'Why,' said Mr Henwick, 'it is reported that Mr Spicer, who is of great influence with the corporation, is not content with the way in which you are said to have used him.'

'He's a d——d ungrateful vagabond. Didn't I get his son-in-law made the postmaster at Physickspring? I must look to this immediately.'

And with that I rose, and took a hackney coach in Palace-yard, and drove straight to the counting-house of Mr Probe, the solicitor, determined to sift this abominable parliamenting to the bottom.

CHAPTER XII

Hot as I was at the House of Commons, I yet had time to cool in some degree between it and Lincoln's Inn Fields, where Mr Probe had his writing rooms – but not quite to an indifference; so when I reached the place, and went in, I found himself there alone, for it was then past four o'clock; and I said to him as soon as I entered,

'Mr Probe,' quo' I, 'what is the meaning of this?'

'I don't know,' replied he; 'what is it that you mean?'

'It is just as well, Mr Probe, to be candid with me,' said I, 'and therefore I request to know the cause of Mr Gabblon having a nefarious correspondence with that unprincipled miscreant, Mr Spicer.'

'Has he?' said Mr Probe.

'That he has, and I want to know all the particulars.'

'Surely you cannot think that I am privy to all Mr Gabblon's correspondence?'

'Do you know, Mr Probe,' exclaimed I, waxing warm, 'that to me it is most unaccountable that he should have this great letter-writing to my borough of Frailtown.'

'I cannot help it,' said Mr Probe; 'the borough is open to any candidate.'

'Do you say so, sir? have not I paid for my seat?'

'Well, sir, if you have, havn't you your seat?'

'But, sir, have not I a right of pre-emption for the next Parliament?'

'I don't recollect that, sir; nothing was said on that head, and of course I could not but do the best for the corporation, with my Lord's permission.'

'And why did you not come to me, sir, before you went to this Mr Gabblon? – I see very well that I have been cheated of my money.'

Upon my saying which he bounced up like a pea in a frying-pan, and said, with a loud voice and a red face, that he didn't know what I meant.

'I thought, Mr Probe,' replied I, with a calm sough, 'that you were a man of more sagacity; but not to waste words, I would just ask if Mr Gabblon is the new candidate?'

'He is,' said Mr Probe calmly; 'and as I am engaged for his interest, you must excuse me for not answering more questions.'

I was dumfoundered to hear a man thus openly proclaim his malefactions, and I turned on my heel and came out of the writing-rooms, a most angry man; and so, instead of returning to the House of Commons, I went straight to the neighbouring chambers of Mr Tough, a solicitor, whom I had observed in a committee as a most pugnacious man, and of whom I said to myself that if ever the time came that I stood in need of an efficacious instrument in a contest, he was the man for my money. Most felicitously, Mr Tough was within, and also alone; and I said to him with a civil smile, 'that I thought it would not be long before I would need his helping hand. You see, Mr Tough,' said I, 'that not being entirely well acquainted with the usages of Parliament, I had not thought proper to make a stipulation with the agent of my borough to give me the first offer at the next election; and, in consequence, he became susceptible – you understand – and has gone over to the side of another candidate: now I want you to be my adviser on the occasion.'

Mr Tough said he was much obliged to me, and that I would not in him put faith in a broken reed. 'But on what ground do you intend to canvass the borough, for much of your chance of success will depend on that?'

'Mr Tough, I am but a 'prentice in the craft of Parliament, and cannot advise a man of your experience; but last year I had gotten a good repute there for a piece of honest business that I did concerning the post-office, by which I made an arrangement most satisfactory to the public, and far better than was expected for the behoof of those more immediately concerned.'

'Oh, I heard something of that, and that Mr Spicer had vowed revenge for the way you had caused a short coming to his son-in-law.'

'Yes, Mr Tough, I understand that for the pains I took to get his gude son that office, which he represented to me was worth nothing, he has rebelled against me; now, as in that affair ye will allow I acted a very public-spirited part, it is not to be supposed that all the corporation will be of his way of thinking.'

'You have, Mr Jobbry, come to me in the proper time; a few days later and all had been lost. But we must bestir ourselves. If you are intent to gain the borough again, you must make a stir this very night; though it is to me a great inconvenience, we must set off together for Frailtown, and pay our respects to the leading members of the corporation; and, to shew our independence, let me suggest to you that our backs must be turned on this Mr Spicer, who certainly has merited the greatest contempt for his conduct.'

The corruption of my nature being up, this advice was very congenial; and I told him to get a chaise, and to come to me at my lodgings by nine o'clock that night, and in the course of the journey we would have time to lay our heads together, and concert in what manner it would be best to proceed.

Accordingly, as there is nothing like despatch and secrecy in getting the weather-gauge of your opponent in an election, I went from Mr Tough's office to the House of Commons, and was there before five o'clock, by which expedition no one suspected where I could have been; and I remained in the House, taking my chop upstairs, and shewing myself well to every one about, so that none could think I was meditating an evasion. I saw Mr Gabblon sitting, well pleased, on the Opposition side; poor, infatuated young man, little suspecting the sword that was hanging by a single hair over his devoted head. Others of my friends saw something of a change about me, and came asking what stroke of good fortune had come to pass that I was looking so blithe and bright? and my answer to them was most discreet, knowing that it was commonly thought I intended to retire from Parliament when the session was over. I said to them that I was only glad to see our weary labours and drowsy night-work drawing to a close; and that Parliament, which I had chosen, in a great mistake, as a place of recreation, had proved far otherwise. Thus it came to pass, that after 'biding in this ostentatious manner in the House till past eight o'clock, I slipped quietly out, and hastening home to my lodgings in Manchester Buildings, had just time to get my *valise* made ready, when Mr Tough, in the post-chaise, came to the door, and sent up his name. Down I went to him with the *valise* in my hand – in I jumped beside him – and away we went. But clever and alert as I was, when the chaise was driving out of Cannon Street, a fire-engine, with watermen and torches thereon, stopped us a little while; and, as it was passing, the flare of the torches cast a wild light in upon us, and, to my consternation, there, in the crowd, did I see the red face and the gleg eyes of Mr Probe, who was standing on the pavement and looking me full in the face, with Mr Tough beside me. This was, to be sure, an astounding thing, and I told Mr Tough of the same; but he made no remark further than saying to the post-boy, in a voice loud enough for Mr Probe to hear, 'Drive straight to the Elephant and Castle.' This was a souple trick of Mr

42

Tough, for it was quite in an opposite direction to where we intended to go; and, as we drove along, when we came to the obelisk in St George's Fields, he again directed the post-boy to make all the haste he could over Blackfriar's Bridge, and get to the north road with the utmost expedition.

CHAPTER XIII

In the course of the journey to Frailtown, we arranged together a very expedient system; and, as Mr Tough said, 'we could not but succeed'. He was really a very clever and dexterous man, and I was so content with what he advised, that, being somewhat fatigued on the second night, I proposed that we should sleep at Beverington, which is a stage short of Frailtown, and which, being a considerable manufacturing town, has a much more commodious inn. To be sure, we might have gone to the hotel at Physickspring, a most capital house; but I had understood that the sedate inhabitants of the borough had no very affectionate consideration for that hotel; and therefore, as it was my business not to give offence to them, I thought it would be just as well to sleep at Beverington, and go on betimes in the morning to the borough.

Accordingly we did so; and in the morning we resumed the remainder of the road, and were not a little surprised, when we were crossing the bridge of Frailtown, to hear vast shouts and huzzas rising from the heart of the town, and to see all hands, young and old, clodpoles and waggoners, all descriptions of persons, wearing purple and orange cockades, and bellowing, like idiots, 'Gabblon for ever!'

My heart was daunted by the din, and Mr Tough was just a provocation by his laughter; especially when, before we got to the Royal Oak Inn, in the market-place, we met a great swarm of the ragamuffins drawing Mr Gabblon and that ne'er-do-weel Probe, in their post-chaise, in triumph, without the horses. The latter, limb of Satan, as he was, had suspected our journey, and had gone immediately to his client; off at once they came from London, and while we, like the foolish virgins, were slumbering and sleeping at Beverington, they had passed on to Frailtown, and created all this anarchy and confusion.

But the mischief did not end with that. The ettercap Probe, on seeing us, shouted in derision, and the whole mob immediately began to halloo and yell at us in such a manner, flinging dirt and unsavoury missiles at us, that we were obliged to pull up the blinds, and drive to the inn in a state of humiliation and darkness. To speak with decorum of this clever stratagem of the enemy, we were, in fact, greatly down in the mouth; and for some time after we got safe into the inns, we wist not well what to do. Gabblon and Probe were masters of the field, and Mr Spicer was their herald every where. At last, Mr Tough bethought him of an excellent device to cut them out; and accordingly he sent for the landlord, and spoke to him if there was nobody in the town who had a grudge at Mr Spicer, and would, for a consideration, befriend us in our need.

There was, to be sure, some hazard in this, as Mr Gabblon and his familiar were likewise inmates of the same inn, and the landlord was, or pretended to be, reluctant to side with either of the candidates. But Mr Tough persuaded him to send for a man whom he said he knew, who bore a deadly hatred to Mr Spicer, and was, moreover, a relation of the Misses Stiches, for whom I had done so much. This man was accordingly brought forward. His name was Isaac Gleaning, an elderly person, and slow of speech, but a dungeon of wit. We received him with familiar kindness; and told him of the misfortune that had over-taken us, by our fatigue constraining us to sleep at Beverington.

'It has,' said Isaac, 'been a great misfortune, for your adversaries have got the ears of the mob, and the whole town is in such an uproar that you must not venture to shew your horns in the street.'

'What then,' said I, 'is to be done?'

'Well,' replied Isaac, 'I have been thinking of that; the players are just now at Physickspring, and they have a very funny fellow among them: could not you send for the manager and the clown, and pay them well to be a mountebank and merry-andrew this evening in the market-place; and get them to throw funny squibs and jibes to the mob, against Mr Gabblon and his compeers?'

Mr Tough rubbed his hands with glee at this suggestion, and no time was lost in sending for the manager: over he came, and we soon privately made a paction with him; whereupon due notice was sent by the bellman through the town, that a great physician from the Athens of the north, with his servant, a learned professor, was to exhibit his skill and lofty tumblings in the market-place.

By the time that the bellman had proclaimed these extraordinary tidings, all the players, tag, rag, and bob-tail, came over from Physick-spring, and set about erecting a stage for their master and the clown in the market-place. They had brought their play-actoring dresses; and they mingled in the crowd with Mr Gabblon's clanjamfrey, insomuch that Macbeth king of Scotland, Hamlet the Dane, and Julius Cæsar, were visible in the streets.

Mr Tough, who was in his way a wag, undertook to instruct Dr Muckledose and his merry-andrew in what they should do; and the whole town was on such tiptoe of expectation, that Mr Gabblon and his friends were in a manner deserted – and the multitude gathered in swarms and clusters round the stage, to secure good places to see the performance. In so far the device was successful beyond expectation, for Mr Gabblon and his coadjutors found themselves obliged to return desjasket to the inn, so much superior were the attractions of the other mountebank.

It was not, however, in this only that the counselling of old Isaac Gleaning was serviceable; he went about among the friends of Mrs Stiches and her late husband, and gathered together about twenty of the topping inhabitants, whom I invited to dinner; and Mr Gabblon and the bodie Probe having engaged themselves to dine with their patron, Mr Spicer, we had a most jovial party.

In the meantime it began to spunk out what a liberal man I was; and the whole mob were as pleased when they heard of the great dinner, as if every one had been an invited guest. Besides, when it was known that the players were hired by me to come over to entertain the town after dark, they in a great body came to the fore part of the inn, and gave me their thanks in three most consolatory cheers. There was, however, a small popular error among them, for I had not bargained for more of the players than the manager and the clown; but Mr Tough, who was a knowing hand, told me not to make two bites of the cherry, but to hire the Mason Lodge, and make the players a compliment for a gratis entertainment of songs and scenes for the edification of the people. This I agreed to do; so that long before the dinner was ready, the wind had changed, and Mr Tough told me to be of good cheer, for we were sailing before it with a steady breeze.

CHAPTER XIV

Frailtown is situated in the centre of Lord Dilldam's estate, and his lordship is in a manner considered the patron of the borough – at least he was so when I got my seat from Mr Curry. It cannot, however, be said that his lordship meddles much in the matter, for he is an easy, plain man; and if the candidates be of good Government principles, he never interferes, but leaves the management of the borough, as a perquisite, to the members of the corporation. In this case between me and Mr Gabblon, he was neutral; for the Whiggery of Mr Gabblon was neither of a deep nor an engrained die, but ready to change as soon as the friends he acted with could get themselves in office, and him a post.

There was a curious thing in the constitution of the borough which well deserves to be mentioned here. By an ancient charter, the corporation consisted of six burgesses of repute, with the mayor at their head; but if, on any occasion of an election of a Member for Parliament, only five councillors happened to be present, and votes were even, the mayor had not a casting vote. To remedy this inconvenience, however, it was ordained, that the mayor should go to the marketplace and summon, at the height of his voice, five burgesses by name, who were of a capacity competent to reckon five score and a half of hobnails; and these five burgesses he was to take with him to the townhall, and they were then and there to give their opinion collectively and individually as to the candidate that should be preferred.

This, it will be seen, was an arrangement fraught with inconvenience, especially in a contest where the candidates had about equal chances; and accordingly, on some occasions it had been the practice at controverted elections to abstract one of the council, and thereby oblige the mayor to put in force the ancient alternative.

Before my visit to Frailtown I had not heard of this abstruse charter, nor had Mr Tough; but when we did hear of it, we were put a good deal to the stress of our ability to determine, when the election would come on, what should be done, especially as there was some risk that the ungrateful Mr Spicer would be the new mayor before the day of election.

'There is no doubt,' said Mr Tough, 'that if he is mayor, the Gabblon party will abstract a councillor, to give Mr Spicer the power of going to the market-cross and summoning five of his own friends whom he will have in readiness there, and thereby secure the election to your adversary; how are we to counteract this?'

'It is perplexing, Mr Tough; for no doubt that regulation in the charter is to secure to the mayor's party always the power of returning the member. But do ye think, Mr Tough, and it's a device that they have never had recourse to, if we also abstract a councillor, the mayor will not have to go to the market-place?'

'That would do,' said Mr Tough, 'that would do; but if we did so, there would then be but five votes; and suppose the council divided, the mayor would make three to our two: it's a very difficult case.'

'Nevertheless, Mr Tough, we'll work on that scantling.'

And accordingly we did so: we did our best to secure as many as we could of the council; and when we had three, our course was plain sailing. But we were more successful – we got four; and yet every one considered our chance of success rendered very doubtful, because it was foreseen that the mayor would have recourse to the ancient usage. But we kept our intention secret, only assuring the people, before we left the town, that on the day of election I would be at my post.

As we had foreseen, Mr Spicer was chosen mayor, and the day of election was appointed in the week following. Mr Tough and I went down the day before, and had a consultation with old Isaac Gleaning, who was quite down-hearted; for he considered that Mr Spicer, by the mayor's privilege, would carry the day, notwithstanding our majority in the council. But when he was informed of our intention to keep back one of our council likewise, a new light broke in upon him.

'To make assurance certain, I would advise you,' said he, 'to try and get one of the Gabblon councillors taken off, and keep your own four on the spot.'

This was not, however, easy to be done; for as the attempt, not the deed, would confound us, it was hazardous to offer a consideration. He, however, undertook to negotiate the business, saying, that he was well acquainted with one of them, a James Curl, who was a hair-dresser. Still, this was a very difficult thing, and greatly tried our wits; but while we were in the perplexity, a young smart man, a friend of the Misses Stiches, came to the town, and presently old Isaac, as we called him, threw out a clever suggestion.

'I'll go,' said he, 'and bring young Tom Brag to you; and as Tom is in his way a blood, give him a sum of money, say five hundred pounds, and bid him go slily to James Curl, and say to James that he has a great bet, in connexion with others, about cutting a particular man's hair in Beverington during the hours of the election; and I suspect, as James is not likely to make so much by the Gabblon job, that he'll take the money.'

Five hundred pounds went to my heart like the sting of an adder; but it could not be helped, and I consented. But, to our great consternation, James Curl would have nothing to do with Tom's wager.* James was an upright patriot, and, as he said himself, in a general election, England expected every man to do his duty, and he was determined to do his. In short, the plan would not take, and we were driven to our wit's end; for, saving James Curl, Tom Brag had no influence nor acquaintance. Late in the evening we were very dull on the subject; at last said Mr Tough:

'We must keep back one of our own men, or find out where their man is to be concealed, for concealed he will be, and constrain him to the town-hall.'

Now, as James Curl was above purchase, it was clear that Aaron Worsted the woolcomber, would be the abstracted; and accordingly it was determined to watch him. Luckily this was resolved upon in good time; for, just as we were speaking, a man came into the room where we were sitting, and brought out of an inner apartment a large bass-viol in a case, which he carried away. The thing attracted no attention at the time; but, very much to our surprise, soon after another man came back with the naked bass-viol, and put it back into the room.

'Ha, ha!' said Mr Tough, 'what tune are they playing, to keep the case and send back the fiddle?'

Old Isaac clapped his hands, and, with a sniggering laugh, said, 'I have caught them. Aaron Worsted is a very small man – he could very easily be stowed in the case; and I'll wager my ears and my eyes that it's for his use that the case has been borrowed.'

And with that he rose; and among some of the servants down stairs he did learn that the case was taken to the house of the mayor, which left no doubt on the subject, but assured us that Aaron Worsted was to be hidden therein. Now, the next thing to be done was to get him, in the case, transported to the town-hall, to be ready in the hour of need to be brought forth; and this was not very easily managed. But just, however, when the council was assembling, and the mayor was in the

---

* A true bill—the facts of the case are even much more honourable than this to a barber and his conscientious old wife.

49

town-hall, by a device of Mr Tough, a countryman, taken from the market-place, went with his cart to Mr Spicer's house, along with a groom of my lord's, a cunning chap, whom, for a guinea and the pleasure of the spree, Mr Tough sent to the mayor's wife, to say that he was come for the bass fiddle that ought to have been sent to the castle that morning. Poor Mrs Spicer, like an innocent daffodil, knowing his lordship's livery, never doubted the message, and consented that the bass-viol should be delivered to him, which was done. But instead of taking his way to the castle, he conducted the cart, with it, to the town hall, and, with the help of the countryman and others, brought up the case and all its contents into the room where we were all assembled, and laid it down on the floor as a musical instrument. But, by some accident, the lid was laid downmost, at which the poor Mr Worsted within was almost suffocated, and began to heave and endeavour to roll about. In short, he was relieved from durance vile, and the election, with a full board, proceeded; so that Mr Spicer, for all his stratagems, was obliged to return me duly elected.

CHAPTER XV

Being much fatigued with the day of election, I was little inclined to make a speech from the window, as the use and wont was; but Mr Gabblon, though he was a mortified man, had still pluck enough to resolve to do so; and accordingly, when the election was declared, he went to one of the windows of the hall, and paternostered to the crowd in a most seditious way, as was to be expected. But they lent a deaf ear to all he said, and he did not make his case a jot the better by it.

For some time while he was speaking, I thought but little of what he said – it was just a bum that went in at the one ear and out at the other; but towards the end I was a little fashed to hear him listened to with sobriety – for he was not without a gift of the gab – and I saw it would be necessary for me to say a few words in return, in the way of offering thanks to the crowd for my election, who, by the way, had as little to say in it as the wild Scot of Galloway.

When the honourable gentleman had finished his oration, I went to the window, very little inclined to be elocutionary; for, as the election cost me a power of money, I could not see wherefore it was to be expected that I should be at any great outlay of words. However, at the incitement of Mr Tough, I went to the window, and there I beheld, when I looked out, a mob of human cattle, such as may be seen at a fair, the major part of whom were plainly not of the town; so I said with great honesty:

'Gentlemen! I'm much obliged to you all for your assistance this day, and more especially for the votes by which you have returned me the representative in Parliament of this borough of Frailtown, and vindicated your privileges. Not one of you but may lay his hand on his heart and declare that you have given a conscientious vote. I therefore most cordially thank you for maintaining the freedom of election and supporting the independence of your member. But, gentlemen, I am not a man of many words; I am a plain man like one of yourselves; the height of my ambition is to resemble my friends. I can say, therefore, no more to convince you of what I feel on this occasion, than that I thank every one of you from the bottom of my soul for the everlasting obligations you have laid me under.'

I then bowed three times, east, and west, and south; and retired from the window amidst a hurricane of applause, the eldest inhabitant of the borough never having heard a speech so much to the purpose.

In so far I was certainly the hero of the day; but the crowning peace of all was shewn to Mr Gabblon. I said to him, in the presence of all who were in the hall, that the contest being now over, we should shake hands as friends; and I held out mine, which he had the good sense to take; and thereupon I invited him and his friends to be of our dinner party, and it is not to be described what an hilarious evening we spent together.

Next morning, when all was quiet, Lord Dilldam, with several of his guests that were at the Castle, came over to the borough, and was prodigiously glad that I was chosen, and invited me and my friends to dine with him. Mr Tough, who was then at my elbow, whispered, 'Decline, decline!' but as I was in a good-humoured vogie mood, I did not perceive the reason of this, and accordingly accepted the invitation; thinking that he would ask Mr Gabblon likewise, and that all would go off in a most agreeable manner.

But when his lordship took his leave and went away, Mr Tough said to me, that he was in doubt if I did right, as the new member, in accepting the invitation; 'for,' said he, 'Lord Dilldam is known, at the Treasury and elsewhere, as the supposed patron of the borough; but you owe him no favour, and therefore you should have been upon your guard; for I would be none surprised if from this scene, it were said that you were my lord's member, and counted by the Treasury as such, more especially as his lordship paid no attention to Mr Gabblon and his friends.'

'We shall see about that,' quo' I; 'his lordship has been very civil in asking me after the fray to come to his house, which I am not loth to do, for I do not think that independence is inconsistent with civility; and therefore, till he makes me a proposition grounded on a sense of obligation, I can see no reason why I should deny myself the gratification of partaking of his hospitality.'

'Well,' said Mr Tough, 'your sentiment is a very good one if you can adhere to it, but we shall see the result by and by: his lordship is a good country gentleman, one of the king's friends; but we'll see what's thought of you and your independence hereafter by the Treasury. You have, however, Mr Jobbry, lost an opportunity of standing forth as an independent man, that days and years may wear away before you again recover the 'vantage ground.'

This remark of Mr Tough disconcerted me at the time, for although he instilled a suspicion into my mind, my easy nature did not allow me to see it was so fraught with danger; but to make a long tale short, we certainly spent a very pleasant day at the Castle. Then I went to Scotland, and put things to right among my affairs there. By that time, the day fixed for the meeting of the new Parliament was drawing near, and I made my arrangements to go to London, to be there at the very opening.

But, guess my astonishment, when by the post before I was ready to set off, down came a letter from the Treasury to me, requesting that I would be present at the meeting of Parliament, as it was understood there was to be a division on the King's speech.

'Oh, ho!' said I, 'the fears of Mr Tough are about to be verified. Of a certainty I will go, and before the meeting I will give a morning call at the Treasury, to ascertain how it is that I am summoned by their circular, being as independent a man as any other in Parliament, and not reverencing the scowl of a minister of state more than my own shadow in the sunshine.'

It would be wrong to say that I was irreconcilably angry with the understrappers at the Treasury, to dare to consider me as one of the bondmen of the Ministers, but I was not well pleased: so the very same day, on my arrival in London, which was the day before the Parliament met, I happened, Heaven knows how it came to pass, to be daunering past the Horse Guards; and I thought to myself I would just step into the Treasury, and ask what particular business was coming on. I did so, and was received in the politest manner possible; which caused me to remark that I had got their circular, a mark of attention I never expected.

'Oh,' said the secretary, 'we are always very particular to the friends of Lord Dilldam; and when his lordship considered you as one of his members, we could do no less than invite the early attendance of one so distinguished for loyalty and independence.'

'I am greatly obliged to you,' said I; 'but I did not know before that I was under a particular obligation to his lordship; however, I will attend the address on the King's speech, and no doubt his Majesty's Ministers will make it a net to catch as many fish as they can; and certainly if, with a safe conscience, I can, I will give it my support; but mind, it's not to pleasure Lord Dilldam, but only my own religious conscience.'

CHAPTER XVI

It is surely a very extraordinary thing to observe at the meeting of every new Parliament how it is composed; but nothing is so much so as the fact that there is a continual increase of Scotchmen, which is most consolatory to all good subjects. Both England and Ireland have many boroughs represented by Scotchmen, but never yet has it been necessary for Scotland to bring a member out of either of these two nations. This, no doubt, is a cause of her prosperity, quite as much as the Union, of which so much is said, and proves the great utility of her excellent system of parish schools.

The remark occurred to me on the night of the first debate, when I looked round the House and saw of whom it consisted; and I said to a friend near me, before the address was moved, that it was a satiafactory sight to see so many very decent men assembled for the good of the nation; and it was an earnest to me that we would have on that night a more judicious division than for many years past. And, accordingly, it was so, for the King's Ministers had cooked their dish with great skill: no ingredient was in that could well be objected to, and it passed unanimously; so that my principles were put to no strain in doing as the other members did. The next important debate was concerning a matter in which some underling of office took upon him to meddle with an election; and, as I don't much approve of such doings, I resolved, though it was a Government question, to vote against Ministers, and to shew, on the first occasion, that I was independent of Lord Dilldam.

The question itself was of no great consequence, nor a single vote either way of much value; but it was an opporunity to place myself on a right footing with Ministers: indeed, after the cost that I had been at for my election, it was not pleasant to think that Lord Dilldam was to get all the credit of sending me into Parliament, and my share of the public patronage likewise. Accordingly, to the very visible consternation of the Secretary of State for the Home Department, the Chancellor of the Exchequer, and two young Lords of the Treasury, who were in a great passion, being rash youths, I was found in the patriotic band of the minority. To be sure they said nothing direct to me, but I could discern that they spoke with their eyes; nevertheless, I was none afraid, and resolved to wait the upshot, which I had not long to do; for, in the course of two days, I received a letter begging my interest for Tom Brag, of Frailtown, who had applied to Lord Dilldam for a particular place, but whom his lordship had declined to assist, having promised to give his patronage to another. As Tom had been useful to me in the election, I was, of course, disposed to serve him; and, more-over, I was glad of such an early opportunity to convince Lord Dilldam that I was not to be counted one of his neck-and-heelers. So I went straight to the Secretary of State for the Home Department, and requested that he would let Tom Brag have the place, which he said he would be very happy to do; but he was greatly surprised at the way in which I had voted the other night, Lord Dilldam's members being always considered as among the firmest supporters of Government.

'That,' quo' I, 'may be very true; I am not, however, one of his, but standing on my own pockneuk: the rule does not apply to me. There is no doubt that I am naturally well-disposed towards his Majesty's ministers, but I must have a freedom of conscience in giving my votes. If you will give the lad Tom Brag this bit postie, I will not forget the favour, – giff for gaff is fair play, and you will find I observe it.'

The Minister looked at me with a queer, comical, piercing eye, and smiled; whereupon I inquired if my young man would have the post.

'It will be proper,' replied the Secretary, 'before I give you a defini-tive answer, that I should have time to investigate the matter.'

'No doubt,' said I; 'but if the place is not promised away, will my friend get it?'

'That's a very home question, Mr Jobbry.'

'It's my plain way, Mr Secretary; and as the place is but a small matter, surely you might give me the promise without much hesita-tion.'

'Yes, Mr Jobbry, that is easily done; but do you know if it would please Lord Dilldam that we gave it to you.'

'I'll be very evendown with you: as an honest man, Mr Secretary, I cannot take it on me to say that the appointment of Tom Brag would give heartfelt satisfaction to his lordship; but I have set my mind on getting the place for Tom; and really, Mr Secretary, you must permit me to think that it's not just proper than an independent member should be refused a civil answer until my lord this or that has been consulted.'

'I beg your pardon, Mr Jobbry. I hope that you have no cause to think I have been uncivil: a system of conciliation and firmness belongs to Ministers on all occasions.'

'True, true,' said I: 'so Lord Sidmouth said would be the conduct of his ministry towards France, and then he went to war with them. But even, Mr Secretary, although you may go to war with me in your conciliation and firmness, as I consider a refusal in this matter would be, it will make no difference in the ordinary questions in Parliament; but you know that, from time to time, the Opposition make harassing motions, in which the good of the nation has no concern, though the felicity of Ministers may. You understand.'

'Really,' replied the Secretary of State, laughing, 'you are a very extraordinary man, Mr Jobbry.'

'I am an honest member of Parliament.'

'I see you are,' was the reply.

'Then if you do, Mr Secretary, you will promise me the place.'

In short, from less to more, I did not leave him till I got the promise; and from that time I heard no more of my Lord Dilldam.

I have been the more particular in this recital, as it was the first occasion on which I had to vindicate my independence; and it was well for me that I did it in a manner so very complete, for soon after there was a change of administration; and had I not done as I did, I must have gone to the right about, and lost every benefit and advantage that induced me to leave my pleasant country improvements in Scotland, to stew myself at the midnight hour with the cantrips of the House of Commons.

But, though this affair was not without the solace of a satisfaction, it was rather an inroad on my system; for, as my object in procuring a seat was to benefit my kith and kin, and to stick a harmless feather in my own cap, I was not quite content to give my patronage to a stranger. Thomas Brag had, no doubt, a claim upon me, and I very readily acknowledged it, especially as it helped to shew me in my true colours; but it would have been far more congenial to my principles had I got the post for a son of my own cousin, whom it would have fitted to a hair. But men in public life, and trafficking with affairs of state, must not expect every thing their own way; so I said nothing, but pocketed the loss, and pruned my wing for another flight, like the hawk in his jesses.

CHAPTER XVII

There is not a more confounding thing in the whole art and system of the British Government than the accident of a change of ministry. To those who are heartily bound, either by principle, ignorance, or selfishness, to the men that have been in power, it is most calamitous; – for those of principle are naturally grieved to see themselves cut off from further ameliorations; the ignorant, not knowing what to do, are as helpless as the innocent babes in the wood; and the selfish are the worst off of all, not being sure if they shall be able to get themselves enlisted by the new set. None are safe on such an occasion but the independent members. Thank Heaven! I was of that corps, and sat still in my place when the change happened. It is very true, that the gentleman who was the Secretary of State when I spoke my mind so freely anent Tom Brag, said to me, on the first night after the change, in a satirical manner, 'that I seemed to find my old seat very comfortable'.

I replied, with a dry dignity, 'that I had a deaf ear, and could only properly understand what was said on the ministerial side of the House'; and I looked very grave as I said this, which caused him to look so likewise, and to redden as if he could have felt in his heart to be angry; whereupon I nothing daunted, added: 'You know, Mr Secretary that was, that I am an independent member, and that it is only the weathercocks that veer about with every wind of doctrine. Depend upon it, Mr Secretary that was, that I am as steady to the point from which the right wind blows as the cock on Kitrone steeple, that the plumber so fastened that it should ever point to the warm and comfortable south.'

'You are a strange man,' said he.

'And you,' said I, 'intend to account me a stranger!'

He was still more confounded; and seeing myself in possession of the advantage, I continued, for it was very impudent of him to notice to me on what side of the House I sat. Wasn't I free to choose?

'And so, Mr Secretary that was'; and I gave him a cajoling wink to mitigate the sarcasm, 'if an impeachment be likely to take place, I will be found at my post and doing my duty.'

This sent him off with his tail between his legs; for there is a great difference visible in the courage of a minister in or out of place and the termagant fellows that rule the roast.

This brief conversation took place in the House, and I saw the eyes of all parties fixed on me; but I was true blue. At the same time I could not but have a sympathy and a sore heart for the humbled and dejected creatures that I saw filling the benches over against me, – so I said to Mr Shiftly, one of those that had come over to our side, that it was a very distressing thing to see men who had been so proud and bold, carrying every thing with a high hand and such lofty heads, not able to get a vote for love nor money, – love, of course, they had none, and as for their money, poor men! notwithstanding their sinecures they were objects of condign pity.

But, besides the claims which the occurrence of a change of ministry has on the tender generosity and compassion of independent members, it is most delightful to observe how the new ministers comport themselves. Being unacquainted with business, they are of course naturally very much averse to receive hints and suggestions; but then they are also wonderfully complaisant; and, as Mr Shiftly, when we were talking on the subject, said to me on this head, 'that all Arabia breathed from the Government offices'.

It might be so; and I will not deny that I had a blandishment of the universal dalliance; but as they became better settled in their seats they grew less and less courteous, and at last hardened down into as cold a marble as their predecessors. Many that had come over to them spoke to me of this official petrifaction; and, to tell the truth, I was not myself without a grudge at the grandeur they began to assume; but as I had an object of my own to serve, I thought it as well to see no more than was just prudent; by which discretion I was soon on as satisfactory a footing with them as I had been with the foregoing set: in sooth, I was rather better; for Lord Dilldam and his own members stuck to the heels of the outs like loch leeches to the old women's legs that wade for them; and it was a marvel among the best informed how I could be so venturesome as to keep my seat, and still sit on the same side of the house. For this I was called Abdiel.

The most grievous thing of all, however, which happens in a change of administration, arises from the complaints that come in from all the airts of the wind against the old ministry, and which are chiefly directed to those members who remain stanch in their independent support of Government. I had my own share of this trouble; and how to manage it in between what was due in justice to the complainants, and what was called for by expediency to my old friends, was most perplexing. At first, I received several petitions and applications with every disposition to look into their merits; but the more I received, and the more I was willing to listen to them, the number increased, till I saw there was no end to it but to shut the doors of impartiality on them all.

For the most part this was a judicious resolution; for, attached to every case was a long story, and if I had not come speedily to the resolution which I did, the whole of my precious time would have been taken up in hearing nothing all the morning but 'wally, wally up yon bank'; and the o'ercome of the same song at night – 'wally, wally down yon brae'.

But let it not be supposed that I was altogether iron-hearted, and would admit no petition, for I had my exceptions to the rule, or rather, I was constrained to have them by my friends, who knew my perseverance when I had a turn in hand, urging me to interest myself, sometimes when the case was very imminent; but, for the most part, really, it seemed to me that men who have causes of complaint are often as unreasonable as those of whom they complain; and it was in consequence of being persuaded of this truth that I resolved to be abstemious in undertaking the redress of grievances and the righting of wrongs. Still, as I say, it behoved me to make, now and then, an exception; but in this I drew a line of distinction, saying to myself, 'It's not possible for a member, be he ever so honest and independent, to take up all cases for the aggrieved; and therefore a discreet man will first make a distinction as to the general class of grievances that he will patronise, and then select particular cases deserving his patronage.' It thus came to pass that I made my selection upon the following principle: First and foremost, I resolved to confine myself to the line of widows and orphans; and accordingly, unless the matter referred to a widow with children, or orphans without parents, it was out of my way. This limited my trouble to a comparatively moderate class, and of that class I limited myself to cases of singular hardship and great distress. It nevertheless happened, now and then, that an importunate petitioner would force me to break through this rule; and, by dint of argument, or the power of persuasion, seduce me to take his part. Instances of this were, however, rare; but the new Ministry had not been many weeks in the saddle, and were going at an easy canter – a Canterbury trot, as easy as Chaucer's pilgrims from the Borough along the Kent road – when a sedate man called on me to advocate his suit. But as it is a story of some length, I must make it the substance of another chapter.

CHAPTER XVIII

Mr Selby was a private gentleman, who had lived in one of the colonies, and who had suffered a great deal in his property by an invasion of the enemy, in consequence of which he was greatly reduced; but his conduct under his distressing circumstances was so exemplary, that the governor, in the king's name, promised that he would be repaid. But many years passed before any thing was done, during which every expedient was put in force to get rid of the obligation to pay him. At last, however, the stubborn truths of the case could no longer be withstood; and a bankrupt dividend was advanced to him, with promises.

The poor man seeing himself so treated, but having still a great affection for Government, bethought him if he could point out a way, and with their consent, by which the requisite fund could be raised, he would be remunerated. This he did, and a very large amount, which did not cost the Government a shilling, was obtained; but, lo and behold, when he applied for the payment of his debt, he was told that the money was appropriated to other purposes!

'Very well,' says he, 'if that be the case, pay me for my trouble in being the means of doing so much public good by getting to you so large a sum of money.'

This was his case; and on my advice he wrote to the minister in whose department the affair lay; but, instead of getting any redress, he got a point-blank refusal, without a word being assigned of any reason for such contemptuous treatment. Thus the man was ruined and driven to beggary, for nothing more was afterwards paid him of his great losses; and he was, in consequence, obliged to become a clerk to a merchant; and what added anguish to his misfortune, he was told that the situation, which had as little to do with Government as the man in the moon, not so much maybe, was ample compensation.

To take up a case of this kind after all had been done that was possible, and to reason in the public offices, and bring it before Parliament by one that was no speaker, required consideration. I was in my humanity well disposed to do what I could for the poor man, and I told him that it would greatly strengthen his cause if he got the opinion of divers other members and acute men to say what they thought of his claim. This, it will be allowed, was judicious advice on my part, inasmuch as I could not see very clearly that it was a matter of law, though it was plainly one of right and justice.

He did so accordingly; and every one who examined his case was of my opinion, and bore the strongest testimony to the fairness of his demand, and the equity of making him a compensation for his trouble: they only differed about what the amount should be. Fortified with these opinions, I then advised him to petition the Honourable House; but at that crisis the change of administration took place, and I thought that as there might be a more lenient spirit in the new Government than had been among those with whom he had formerly to deal, I said to him, we would stop going forward with his petition, and apply to the new ministers.

Thus it came to pass that I was myself, in the end, rendered accessary to a very cruel transaction. The poor man's means had been in a great measure exhausted by his losses; but, still flattered by hope of ultimate redress, he kept on his way in an even tenor, until all the relics of what he had were nearly exhausted, and his time spent thriftlessly. In these circumstances I went to the new minister and stated his situation, but days and weeks passed without an answer; and at last, when one was given, it was to the same effect as the former; and Mr Selby, with his family, were in consequence utterly undone. I did not, however, think so, or rather, I wished to think otherwise, and advised him still to go to Parliament; but he remarked, 'that although moderate disappointment is sometimes a spur to endeavour, continual disappointment never fails to break the heart. I have not the means left of going to Parliament, for justice has its money-price in England; nor can I afford the time: my case, I apprehend, is not uncommon, but it is not the less hard to me.'

I was very sorry to hear him say this, and comforted him, as well as I could, with hopes that I well knew were as empty as blown soap-bells and bubbles; and it cut my tender feelings very much when he said: 'Mr Jobbry, I am greatly obliged to you for your friendliness in this matter; but adversity is an eye-salve; and when distress comes, good subjects grow scarce.'

I inquired what he meant, and he replied, 'I think, sir, if you look at my case, both first and last, you will see that I have cause to say, that there is no sedition in being of opinion that a reform is wanted in the British Government.'

'Wheesht! Mr Selby, – wheesht! you must not allow yourself to hint of such a thing.'

'I cannot help it, Mr Jobbry; I am only sorry to see that the roaring multitude make a sad mistake in the question, crying out for reformation in Parliament, when the whole ail and sore is in the withers and loins of the executive government.'

'What do you mean, Mr Selby?'

'Only this, – the business of all governments is to enforce the law, but their own practice is to regard its principles as little as possible; and thus all reforms are but changing words, until governments are as much bound towards their subjects by principles as one individual is to another. It cannot, however, be long endured, that governments may continue to do only their own will, and have no respect for justice unless it happens to be supported by parliamentary influence. A man of a just and high mind, who will trust to his rights, and not to the interference of his friends, has no chance, under the existing system, of getting even a moiety of justice.'

'Hoot, toot, toot! Mr Selby, ye must not speak in that manner.'

'I have reason, Mr Jobbry. To be sure, the atom which an individual is in a great state may seem an insignificant thing in the view of those that sit in high places; but the poor beetle that we tread upon feels as much in its anguish as the giant. Till Governments, and Houses of Commons, and those institutions which the sinful condition of man renders necessary, are made responsible to a tribunal of appeal, whose decisions shall control them, there can be no effectual reform. The first step is to take away all will of its own from Government – for statesmen are but mere men, rarely in talent above the average of their species, from what I have seen – and oblige it to consider itself no better than an individual, even with respect to its own individual subjects. Let the law in all things be paramount, and it will little matter whether the lords or the vagabonds send members to Parliament; at least, it is my opinion that it will not be easy to find five or six hundred gentlemen much better than the present members of Parliament.'

'That's a very sensible remark, Mr Selby.'

'Nor,' continued he, 'is it likely that half a million of electors will make a better choice than a smaller number. In fact, the wider the basis of representation is spread, the greater will be the quantity of folly that it will embrace: and we have only to look at the kind of persons whom the multitude send to Parliament, to anticipate what will be the character of a reformed house. Look at the moiety of Westminster, for example.'

'All that may be very true, Mr Selby; and I am glad to hear that ye're not a reformer.'

'I beg your pardon; I am a very firm one, but not of the parliamentary sort. I desire to see the law purified and exalted, that mankind may enjoy the true uses of government – protection. But it was a wish and an aim – it is so no longer.'

With these words he went away; but there was a tone of sorrow and anger in my remembrance of them, like the scent of sour in a vessel that has been used for holding sweet ingredients; and I was for some time very uneasy. Soon after, I met him in the street a very altered man. I stopped, and kindly inquired how he was.

'As well as can be expected,' said he.

'You don't look so.'

'No,' said he; 'because the disappointment is working to its effect. At my time of life it is not easy to learn a new way of living to what I have been accustomed to – new friends, new habits – all the world a-new – especially when to privation is added a galling sense of wrong – contumely in return for good.'

'Oh! you must not let yourself think that way; it will only make your distress greater.'

'I intend it should do so,' said he, sternly: 'I only wish it would do it a little more quickly.'

He then went away, and I never again saw aught of him; but in due time I shall recite the sequel.

CHAPTER XIX

The concern of Mr Selby troubled me a great deal; for although I could see that he was fully entitled to a handsome recompense, there was yet evidently a rule applied against him of an unsatisfactory kind. For the man himself I was sincerely grieved, because, as he had rendered a service which could not be denied, it seemed to me that something must be rotten in the state of Denmark which allowed the time and ingenuity of any man to be taken from him without a compensation, especially as John Bull is a free payer of all that do him any good. From the impression that Mr Selby had made upon me, I began to turn my mind more on the frame and nature of our Government; for although I went into Parliament with the full intention of administering my share of the Government patronage with judgment and sensibility, and to keep aloof as much as possible from political matters, particularly of those that related to France and foreign countries, I yet saw that there was some jarring and jangling in the working of the State, that was not just agreeable. Thus it happens that knowledge grows upon us; but when I came to reflect that the choice of the limbs and members of Government is naturally limited to a very few, who, from their station in society, have not the best opportunities of acquiring a right knowledge of the world, my opinions underwent a change; and I soon perceived a wide difference between reverence for the Government, and attachment to the men of whom it is composed.

'Every government,' said I to myself, one night when I came home early from a drowsy wrangle of a committee on the estimates – 'Every government is a sort of machine, that is naturally formed out of the habits, morals, and manners of its respective people. We in this country are fond of monarchy: in no country do people know their respective situations with regard to one another so well as in this. Indeed, I have heard most intelligent men in India say, that the order of castes, though of a different kind, prevailed as strikingly in England as among the Hindoos; and certainly the sense of subordination in the different degrees of life is here very perfect: even Nature seems herself to minister to this; for just look at the stout, short, civil, spirited little men that she breeds for grooms and servants, and compare them with the tall, lank, genteel aristocracy of their masters. To follow out the comparison to the different orders of society would not be consistent with my plan: it is only indeed necessary that I should advert to the natural cause that produces the political effect. We are plain and palpably to the sight a nation disposed to a monarchical form of government, and I have no doubt that where other kinds of governments prevail, other sorts of people will be found. This fact granted, as it must be, and the choice of rulers being limited to a small number, it must of course come to pass that talent – which nature does not seem to give out to ranks, like physical peculiarity – will, as it has ever been, be distributed among the community at large. There are not distinct races of genius, which does not procreate, as there are races of horses and dogs; and thus it happens, that from time to time the natural class from which the government is formed is obliged to borrow talent from the inferior classes. It is, however, not a very safe and solid thing: when this is requisite, it either betokens mutations and revolutions, or is an effect of them.'

This very well-considered opinion of mine has grown into an article of faith; and yet it has not made me greatly content with a very common practice among those who, by their station, are entitled to bear the bell in the Government, namely, that of their too frequent custom of sucking the brains of their inferiors, and casting away the rind. But still, though it is a custom that cannot but be condemned, it rises, I fear, out of circumstances that are beyond the control and measures of man. It no doubt breeds discontent: the sappy brains that are sucked without being paid for, grow acrid and sour, and, like rotten oranges in a box, they infect their neighbours; and thus it often is, that those to whom governments are most obliged, become their most dangerous and evil subjects, inasmuch as from them proceed those acrimonious opinions that, sooner or later, corrode the established well-being of the state.

But although it is very fit that I should here describe the course of reflection into which the unjust and ill usage that Mr Selby suffered led me, his was not the only case of the kind that tended to rivet my opinion: several others soon after occurred; and although none of them could be said, like his, to be a claim for reward in consequence of success, yet all and every one of them were for authorised services of an experimental kind, in which the remuneration was withheld.

To what conclusion this course of thought might have led me, I cannot determine; – certainly never to have sided with those who were diffusing the delusion, that a redress of the causes of discontent was to be effected by giving the unenlightened many, an increase of dominion over the enlightened few. Governments are things of nature, and cannot be changed nor removed but by the progress of seasons and time, except with great confusion. They are like hills—— However, my meditations were interrupted rather abruptly; for, not meddling myself overly with even our home politics, I was roused out of what I would call my easy acquiescence with the proceedings of Government, by a sudden dissolution of Parliament. Some difference on a speculative question caused a division in the cabinet, and the new ministry appealed to the people, as it is called: I had therefore to cleek Mr Tough in my arm and hurry away to Frailtown; where I was told that Lord Dilldam, though an excellent quiet country gentleman, was so offended at my adhering to the opponents of his party, that he was determined to oust me from the borough.

CHAPTER XX

I had an apprehension that my abiding on the Treasury side of the House, at the change of ministry, was not agreeable to Lord Dilldam, and was therefore none surprised when informed of his determination to throw the weight of his influence against me in the election; insomuch that I had begun to have some conversation with Sir Abimelech Burgos, who was proprietor of three boroughs in the West; but the suddenness of the dissolution broke off the negotiation, and, upon the advice of Mr Tough, a real clever man at an election job, I resolved to try my own luck again at Frailtown.

When we reached the borough – and I took care on this occasion not to slumber nor sleep by the way – we drove at once to the Royal Oak; and Mr Tough, with most excellent dexterity, agreed with the landlord that we should have the use of the whole house for a certain sum of money.

This was a very capital stroke of policy; for as all the other public houses in the town were of a mean order, he considered that Mr Gales, my lord's new candidate and kinsman, would make his head-quarters at the grand hotel in Physickspring; because he was a beau that dressed nicely, and was in all things dainty and delicate. But the main reason that Mr Tough had in driving Mr Gales to that hotel was, a dislike which the inhabitants of Frailtown bore to the upsetting garish pride of every thing about Physickspring.

'It may seem,' said Mr Tough, 'that this is a trifling matter, considering the close corporation and singular constitution of the borough; but the generality of mankind, unconsciously to themselves, are governed by public opinion; and we may rest assured, that the populace will not be satisfied with Mr Gales, and that their dissatisfaction will more or less tell on the town council.'

I thought his remark very shrewd, but we had both great fears of my success; for that inveteracy, Mr Spicer, was mayor a second time; and old pawky Isaac Gleaning was in an ailing way, and could not give the effectual assistance that I received from him, for a consideration, at the former election: so, after we had paid a few visits together, I came home to the Royal Oak rather in a subsiding mood, and had just said to Mr Tough, in meditative sobriety, that

'The troubles which afflict the just
In number many be;'

when who should come into the room, to pay me his respect, but that ramplor young fellow, Tom Brag, that I had got the post so cleverly for.

His office was not in Frailtown, but in the neighbouring more considerable place of Beverington: no sooner, however, had the thankful lad heard of my arrival, than he came over in his gratitude to offer me his services. He was a prize; for although he had no great weight with the town council, he had a supple hand at a trick. It was not, however, my business to be seen in any thing of the sort; so I left Mr Tough and him to concoct their own stratagems; and, in the mean time, being perfectly independent, I did not think it necessary to shew myself under any particular reverence for my Lord Dilldam. Accordingly, just as a matter of course, I threw myself into a post-chaise, and drove over to pay my respects in an ordinary civil manner at the Castle. His lordship, at the sight of me, was in the greatest consternation, especially when I said to him: 'My lord, although me and Mr Gales are likely to have a rough tussle in the oncoming election, there can be no reason why I should not continue to behave with decorum and respect to your lordship.'

'In truth, Mr Jobbry,' was his reply, 'I never thought, from the ease with which I allowed you to carry the election last time, that you would have made so light of that favour.'

By this short speech I got some insight into his lordship's character, and could see that, although he was a most respectable nobleman, consistent in his principles and moderate in his public temper, yet he had not an ill conceit of himself; – so I said, touching my lips as it were with honey, that 'it was a great pity I did not rightly understand the potentiality of his lordship in the borough; and that I was not a politician, but a sober domestic member, attending chiefly to the local improvements of the kingdom, only voting on occasional political questions with ministers; and, really, that I had thought his lordship's great experience of business in Parliament would, without any explanation, have satisfied him that changes in the heads of the Government were but secondary matters with the like of me; my great end and purpose being to get my own obligations to the public righteously performed, which could not be done if I veered about from side to side like a party man.'

On hearing this, his lordship looked most well pleased; and said, 'that my principles did me honour as a man, and that it was to be regretted we did not understand each other better; for,' continued he, 'it was not so much because you gave in your adherence to the new ministers that I objected, as it was because you were supposed to act independent of me.'

'My lord,' said I, feeling the full force of what he said, 'misunder-standings will arise between the best of friends; and I am very sorry to say that, to all appearance, I am likely soon to repent I was not so con-junct with your lordship.'

'Yes, Mr Jobbry, you may have cause to repent; for now you will feel the force of my influence; and you may be assured that I shall leave no means untried to secure the borough for my young relation, Mr Gales. At the same time, Mr Jobbry, I will do you the justice to ac-knowledge, that had a better understanding existed between us, I would not have allowed Mr Gales to oppose you; for, although he made some figure at college, – he's an excellent classical scholar, and can compose and deliver speeches of great promise, – he is not exactly the sort of man that I would have chosen; for I want a man of business among those whom I make the depositaries of my influence.'

In short, his lordship and me became very couthy, and he said 'he would return my visit next day; for that in all things he thought we should act as honourable rivals for the love of that fair damsel, the borough of Frailtown, (an unproductive old maid, or rather unmarried lady,) and seek to win her smiles and favour by our chivalry, maintain-ing a mutal courtesy towards each other.'

So far my visit to the Castle was auspicious; and when I returned to the borough, I told Mr Tough what had passed; upon which he laughed, and said, – 'In the desperation of our circumstances, you cannot do better than so continue the war in the enemy's territory; for, to tell the truth, your protogee, Tom Brag, is not very sanguine in his opinion of our success; but the fellow has great tact, and he tells me that our only chance lies in annoying Mr Gales personally, so as to disgust him with the borough; for he is morbidly sensitive, and is easily molested by a small trifle. Now, your tactics are to conciliate my lord, and I have settled with Tom Brag that his are to annoy Mr Gales, which we are in the better condition to do by having the commonalty on our side, and by taking up our residence in this plain homely manner in the town.'

I agreed that the view which Mr Tough had taken of the state of my case was very judicious; and accordingly we arranged to act upon what I called the double-dealing principle, – for really it was so, both in its morality and practice. But men have a license in the time of a general election, and I availed myself of no more than the common privileges of the saturnalia.

CHAPTER XXI

I am, of course, having been the candidate, not very well acquainted with the devices which had been concerted between Thomas Brag and Mr Tough; I heard, however, that, among others, they agreed to keep in their pay a gang of skittle-players, fearless, ne'er-do-weels, who were kept constantly on the ree with ale and strong liquor, and were to hold themselves in readiness for any exploit at a moment's call.

With these, accordingly, when my lord returned his visit next day, in great pomp, with four horses and outriders, and yet without Mr Gales' cockade, the phenomenon attracted public wonder; and, somehow, Tom Brag's skittle-players got an inkling of the business, and during his lordship's visit they gathered round the inn-door, with all the ragamuffinry of the town, shouting and making a fearful noise. I could see, when my lord heard them, that he was a little disturbed; but I told him how I had quietly allowed it to be known that his lordship's visit to me was entirely of a friendly nature, and therefore I wished that it should not be mixed up with the business of the election.

'That was most considerate of you, Mr Jobbry,' said his lordship, 'and I might just have expected so from a man of your sagacity; and therefore I hope you will come in a friendly manner and dine with me at the Castle tomorrow.'

'Your lordship has a fine taste,' said I; 'and certainly nothing will give me more pleasure; but since you have condescended to put our intercourse upon that dignified footing, I will only make one condition.'

'Well,' said his lordship, 'it is granted, without knowing what it may be.'

'My Lord Dilldam,' quo' I, 'in doing so, you have only shewn the courtesy of your own nature, and paid me what I feel to be a great compliment. The condition, therefore, that I propound, is one that I humbly hope will be congenial to your lordship's own benign nature: I but request that you will invite Mr Gales and his friends to be of the party; and that all about it shall be of the same conciliatory and chivalric description.'

'You have plucked the idea from my own head,' said his lordship;

'I was just about to propose the same thing; I only hesitated lest you should think I was taking too great a liberty.'

'My dear lord,' said I, 'liberty! – it is an honour that I was diffident to propose.'

We accordingly shook hands in the most cordial manner. I saw him to the steps of his carriage, assisted him in, and expressed to him, as the door was about to be shut, how deeply I felt the honour of his visit. At these words, Tom Brag, who was in the crowd, gave me a knowing wink, and presently his skittlers and the crowd gave three cheers, and his lordship drove away, as proud as a cock on his own dunghill.

Presently after, Mr Tough came to me to hear what had passed, and I told him; at which he really chuckled with delight, requesting me to ask no questions; but adding, 'that Tom Brag was, for a trick, the very eldest born of Beelzebub.'

Just while we were speaking, it came to pass that Mr Gales came riding with great pomp and pageantry; but as the Little-good would have it, Tom Brag's crew – as if to shew a distinction between the scented classical young man and his lordship – gave enfeoffment of the borough, as the Scotch lawyers say, with yird and stane – that is, they pelted him with all manner of abominations from the street, till they made him a perfect object, and sent all his coadjutors after him in whirlwinds of mud, yelling and yelping out of the town.

What was to be done for this uproar? It was clear that his lordship, in his visit to me, had been received with every demonstration of the greatest respect; but the treatment of his candidate was a proof, beyond all doubt, that it was not his lordship, but the candidate, that was unpopular.

'You must,' said Mr Tough to me, with as grave a face as he could possibly put on, 'reprimand Tom Brag for not checking this ebullition of popular fury, and send at once to his lordship to express your regret at this untoward action.'

'I will leave the matter,' said I, shaking my head, (whether I smiled or frowned, the reader may guess) 'entirely to you, Mr Tough; but be sure and make it plain to his lordship's understanding how displeased I am that my party should have manifested such a spirit against his lordship's candidate, while they treated himself with so much respect.'

This was no sooner said than done. Tom Brag, who was himself the very head and front of the offending, was dressed in his best in a jiffy, mounted on his horse, and away to Dilldam Castle, with my compliments; where he did not remain long, but came back to me before my consternation was half over, and told me the many kind things his lordship had said to him concerning my character, and how he thought that if every contested election in the kingdom was managed in the same spirit of candour and fairness, how very little trouble there would be; that as for what had happened to Mr Gales, it was a thing to be expected; and that party spirit, he could himself see, ran high in the borough, but it was only among the lower orders; thank God! the candidates, as principals, had no share in the licentiousness of the mob.

An elder of the kirk of Scotland, from behind the plate on the Lord's day, could not have told his tale with more decorum than that unreverent young man, Tom Brag; but it was with a great difficulty that I could reply to him in a becoming manner; so I only shook my head, at the which he ran out of the room as if he would have died of laughter.

'Now,' said Mr Tough, who was present, after Tom had gone away, 'you have made a good lodgment with my lord, let us not lose the advantage, for it is our only chance. That acrimonious fellow, Mr Spicer, the mayor, is all alive and awake to the manner in which his power under the charter may be exerted: we shall not be able to counteract him; he has already settled who are to be the five good men and true that he is to summon from the market-place, all firm adherents of his own. At the same time, he calculates that there will be no need to have recourse to that alternative; but I have heard that, since my lord's visit to you, he has been looking a little black. You must therefore, as your only chance of carrying the borough, establish yourself well with his patron, my lord.'

'Never fear,' quo' I, 'a nod and a wink are both alike to a blind horse: but what shall we do, Mr Tough, even were his lordship brought over to my side, if this ungrateful devil be so against us, either in the council or by the five good men and true?'

'Trust to Providence, and do your best,' cried Mr Tough.

This shews to what desperation our cause was reduced.

CHAPTER XXII

Next day I was ready betimes to go to the Castle, where it was publicly understood that I was to dine; and when I set out I was attended by a great retinue of the commonalty. In going along I saw behind a clump of trees an assemblage of men and boys having Mr Gales's cockades in their hats: the sight daunted me, but the crowd that was round my carriage gave them three cheers; and as I happened just at the moment to discern among them Tom Brag in a smock-frock, my dismay cleared off like a cloud in a May morning; and I drove on cheerfully to the Castle.

It was well I did so; for soon after, Mr Gales came in full puff in his barouche; and the crowd, coming from the plantation, received him with shouts, and laughter, and great applause. He seeing that they wore his colours, was greatly delighted; and a proud man was he when he saw them take the horses from his carriage, and bidding the servants get down, dragged him along, like captivity leading captive.

He thought they were drawing him in triumph to Castle Dilldam; but, to his astonishment, they took another road, and drew him into a pool in the river, where, wishing him good day, they left him sitting in his horseless carriage, cooling his heels, till his servants could get him out.

The servants were not, however, long in coming up, and, with the assistance of Tom Brag and his skittlers, they made haste to draw the carriage from the pool; but, by some accident, it so happened that in this business the carriage was overset, and Mr Gales tumbled headlong into the water, where he would have been drowned but for the presence of mind and ready hand of Tom, who caught him just in time by the cuff of the neck, and dragged him, more dead than alive, to the shore.

Such is the account that I received of the disaster; but what happened at the Castle, and which was within my own knowledge, requires me here to make a more circumstantial recital.

Lord Dilldam was very energetic on points of punctuality connected with his dinner-hour; and accordingly, as he had for the occasion assembled many of his neighbours, he was vexed that Mr Gales did not come at the time appointed. We sat down to dinner, and still he was not forthcoming. It was not, however, my business, considering the object in view, to take much pains to appease his lordship's displeasure, and therefore I said,

'It was surprising that Mr Gales, who knew our party was one of reconciliation, should neglect to come.'

I saw that my remark troubled his lordship still more, and it was soon visible to the whole company that he was an angry man.

A short time after dinner Mr Gales made his appearance, and his reception was not one of the most cordial kind.

He excused himself by stating, rather, I must say, with good humour, in what way he had been deceived by the false colours of Tom Brag and his party.

'Pooh, pooh!' cried Lord Dilldam, 'don't excuse your own heedlessness: you ought not to have been deceived by a mere electioneering trick. What would rescued Europe and the British nation have thought of the sagacity of the Duke of Wellington at the battle of Waterloo, had he been deceived by Napoleon dressing his army in scarlet like the English soldiers?'

Mr Gales, who was still a little disturbed, replied,

'Upon my honour, my lord, I do not see much fitness in the comparison.'

'I daresay not, and that makes your inattention the more palpable; for the numbers you had to contend with were a mere trifle compared to the thousands on that illustrious day. In fact, Gales, I am not pleased. This was an occasion on which the political tranquillity of the county depended; and if your condition was really such that you were obliged to go back to Physickspring, you might have sent one of your fellows to apprise me of your disaster.'

Here I thought fit to edge in a pacifying word:

'My lord,' said I, 'you must excuse Mr Gales under such a comical misfortune; for every one would not, in such circumstances, have been able to preserve his self-possession. No doubt, self-possession during a debate in the House is——'

'Yes,' said his lordship, 'I know it; and it is that – the want of self-possession – that makes me the more grieved, sir; it is the first quality in a Member of Parliament – eloquence is but the second; and a man possessed only of eloquence, without self-possession, is very apt to make a fool of himself.'

The rector of the parish, Dr Bacon, who was there, remarked that his lordship had made a philosophical observation. It was plain, however, that the harmony of the company was broken, and that Lord Dilldam was in no very good humour with his candidate. Indeed, it was quite evident that a very little persuasion would have induced his lordship to cast him off; and it was equally obvious that Mr Gales himself did not think very complacently of his part in the election drama. Indeed, a hope began to dawn in my bosom that they would quarrel, and that I should only have to walk the course. However, nothing happened that night; and I returned to the borough, after having spent a most agreeable evening; for, although my lord's temper was in a state of erysipelas, I could not, without a breach of truth, say that it did not give me satisfaction. This was increased when, on my return, I saw a great light shining from the market-place, and on approaching the Royal Oak, beheld the front illuminated with letters made of wine-glasses fastened by strings, with small lighted wicks in each, like lamps, displaying the words, in great splendour, 'RECONCILIATION – DILLDAM AND JOBBRY FOR EVER,' – and all the town ranting and revelling before the door.

At first I thought this was a little too much; but when Mr Tough laughingly told me that it was a suggestion of his own, I knew it was not without sagacity.

'In truth,' said he, 'this is not a time for modesty. We must make the most we can of your visit to my lord: it has already abashed our adversaries. Mr Gales, it is known, damned the borough when he was pulled out of the water, and threatened to give up the contest. If we are to be defeated, let us not fall without a struggle.'

I then told him what had passed at dinner; upon which he said, 'All works well; and before the mob disperses, we shall circulate a story about the quarrel of my lord and Mr Gales: no particulars will be given, but only that there has been a quarrel, – the imagination of the populace will soon supply particulars.'

CHAPTER XXIII

The young stand by principle, the old by law, the wise by expediency, and the foolish by their own opinion. Much of this truth was visible in the controversies of our election. All the youth of the town were next morning on my side, – the elderly persons did not approve of such a departure from ancient custom, as the countenance which they thought Lord Dilldam gave to me against his own candidate, – and the judicious few were of opinion that one of the candidates should withdraw; it being of little importance which, for any good the borough was to get by either: but the great bulk of the people had declared themselves for me, and were determined to support me through thick and thin.

Such was the report of the state of public opinion I received in the morning. 'But,' said Mr Tough, when he had made it, 'the aspect of all things is brightening. Your most determined enemy, Mr Spicer, is indisposed, and confined to bed: his disease, I have no doubt, comes of the reported quarrel between my lord and Mr Gales; and he is mortified that he may be required by Lord Dilldam to support you. I suspect, from the pride and pertinacity of the man, that he will rather remain at home ill than attend the election. I think we have the ball at our foot. If he absents himself tomorrow, the great day, from the townhall, then the oldest counsellor must go to the market-cross and summon five good men and true; and if he do not, then the next senior counsellor must go. Now the senior counsellor is a weak, old, infirm man, not at all likely, in the present excited state of the town, to venture to the market-place; and the next counsellor is stanch to our party, and will readily do the duty; I shall, therefore, instruct him on the subject, and he will call by name five who will serve our purpose, and whom I shall have ready on the spot.'

Greatly, however, to our surprise, next morning no new occurrence had taken place. Mr Spicer was charming well again, and every thing wore a frown to my cause. The multitude from all parts of the country round poured into the town in flocks, to conserve their rights and privileges; but no message nor tidings were heard either from the Castle or Mr Gales; yet Mr Spicer was courageous, and went buzzing about as brisk as a bee.

I did not like, nor did Mr Tough like, the ominous silence of no messenger from the Castle, nor forerunner from Mr Gales: we were confounded; for this sudden secession of Lord Dilldam was inexplicable, and the conduct of Mr Gales was irreconcilable with his interests as a candidate; and yet the bravery of Mr Spicer, the mayor, in this uncertainty, was equally unaccountable.

Mr Tough and I were thus reflecting together, when suddenly starting up, he exclaimed, 'The day may be our own, but ask no questions.'

Out of the room he instantly ran; and Tom Brag, on horseback, was soon seen galloping on the road to the Castle.

'What is he about?' said I to Mr Tough; who only replied, 'Ask no questions.'

In a short while after, we went through the shouting multitude to the town-hall together, where we beheld, to our dismay, the mayor and council assembled; and Mr Gales, who had come in by a back door, fearful of outrage, standing at Mr Spicer's right hand.

'We are undone,' whispered I to Mr Tough. 'Not yet,' said he, panting with awe and dread.

Then an officer being about to open the courts to begin the business, a cry got up that an express had come from my lord, with a letter to the mayor. Who brought that letter was never known to me; for the hall being crammed with spectators, and surrounded by the populace, it was handed over head from one to another till it was delivered.

The mayor on receiving it opened it with a trembling hand. It was a note with Lord Dilldam's compliments – then some unreadable words – then 'hoping' – and then other unreadable words – then 'interested,' – and other unreadable words; – concluding with, 'that the election of Mr Jobbry had taken place'; thereby, as it seemed, intimating that he was interested in me alone.

Mr Spicer shook like the aspen, for the job was odious to him; and presently he complained of being suddenly taken unwell, cried out for fresh air, and was with difficulty assisted out of the room. Upon this, Mr Tough, all of a tremble, cried out that the business of the election must proceed according to law, the charter of the town having provided for such accidents.

'In the king's name,' cried he, waxing bolder, 'I demand of you, Mr Idle, as senior counsellor, to go into the market-place and summon five good men and true, burgesses of this borough, to repair with you to this place, to assist the council in the election of a member.

'Dear me, dear me!' cried Mr Idle; 'I am an aged man; I cannot do that: I am in such a flutter that I can scarcely recollect my own name, far less five others.'

'Then,' cried Mr Tough, 'the senior of the council having refused, on the plea of inability, to perform the duty, it belongs to you, John Gnarl, to perform it, and without delay, for the business of the election has now commenced.'

John Gnarl, with an evident inward laugh, made no bones of the business, but alertly starting up, he went forth from the hall; all the crowd giving passage to him as he passed, amazed at this high solemnity, which had not been performed in the memory of man; and on reaching the cross, he there summoned five burgesses by name and craft, who, greatly to the astonishment of all present, were accidently standing together, dressed in their Sunday clothes; and back John came to the hall with them behind him.

When the names of the two candidates, Mr Gales' and mine, were read over, the whole five burgesses, without even speaking to one another, unanimously advised the council to elect me – which was a very extraordinary electioneering coincidence.

Mr Gales looked aghast; but his lawyer, a genteel young man, peremptorily told him it could not be avoided: the charter had established the principle, and Mr Jobbry was duly elected.

While this little fracas was going on, I saw Mr Tough quietly lift my lord's note from the table, which the mayor had in his consternation left, and putting it in his pocket, began to chew bits of paper out of the same pocket; but whether they were fragments of the note or not, I could take my Bible oath as to my ignorance of the fact.

Thus was I a second time *elected* the independent representative of Frailtown.

CHAPTER XXIV

The aspect of a new Parliament after a change of administration is very comical. On the left side there is stern and vindictive frowns; and on the right, exultation and complacency, interspersed with young unknown visages, of a serious senatorial cast, prognosticating oratory. It is a lucky thing, however, for the country, that the number of these and other speakers is comparatively very few; for at the best they are but a necessary evil, and only help the more sagacious editors of the newspapers to make wiser reflections. The prudent, those that set a watch on the door of their lips, never speak at all, or, at the most, only put a young man right when he happens, in the warmth of debate, to be caught tripping in a Parliamentary fact. – But I have less to do with the House than with what happened to myself in and about it.

Whatever resolution a member may form for the guidance of his conduct on first entering Parliament, he will see, as he grows familiar with its usages, that he is constrained by some inscrutable power to conform very generally in all things to the conduct of his neighbours.

I have already said, that the House of Commons is a peculiar community; and every day that I belonged to it, I was the more and more convinced of this truth. Out of doors men are regulated by public opinion, in their thoughts, their actions, and their enterprises; but within the walls of that House there is a different atmosphere; members become less and less susceptible of the influence of public opinion, and more and more to the dogmas of Parliament, which the populace, with their usual wisdom, always think are less sound than their own.

I make the remark, because when I took my seat after the election which has just been described, I felt myself elevated above many persons that I saw around me, whom I had previously considered as in some things my superiors; – if I were to feign candour, I would say in all things; but I adhere to the conclusions of my own understanding.

This consciousness of superiority puzzled me a good deal; but I soon saw that it proceeded from the same sort of thing that gives men an advantage over one another in the world, and which often passes for superior understanding. I had only, by being a member of that peculiar community, learned some of those sleights of art inherent in it, similar

80

to those which give men a power over mankind in the world, and like-wise often passes for talent. Although, therefore, it could not be said that I was a distinguished Member of Parliament – my name was never seen in the debates in the newspapers – I yet discovered that I was accounted one of a clever sort, especially among my junior brethren; and thus it came to pass, that I was bit by bit solicited from my own determination, and, without becoming a partyman, to have a leaning towards those who were more inveterately touched with the patriotism of making long speeches.

For the first session, I know not how it happened, probably in consequence of the Parliament being new, and expectants having in the new members more quarry, I was less troubled with applications for patronage than ever before; but I lost something of my relish for regulating the distribution of what posts I did get: in truth, I ought not to take great credit to myself for this, as the Government was quite as much the cause, fancying that if a young man got a post, the emolu-ments of which he allowed to be taxed with an annuity, – for example, to the widow of his predecessor, – it was opening a door to corruption, by uniting the widow's interests with his. The custom was, therefore, stopped, and the officer received his full emoluments.

I remember very well, that this at the time was thought a notable reform, and it was very acceptable to the people at large: but I had my doubts of its practical wisdom; for if a man could afford to give an annuity out of his emoluments, surely he could have paid as much back to the state, and thereby caused an important item of savings; for, be it observed, by the new arrangement the poor widow was left destitute, and became in so much a cess upon her friends, who of course became discontented. I have often wondered how an auld-headed old friend of mine, that then was in office, should have consented to such a frus-tration of the widow's hope, without making the public benefit by the alterations, especially as he was a Scotchman.

I have no respect for such nugatory regulations; and I trust my public conduct warrants me to say, that concerning the same, great delusion beguiles the world; for although I have ever been a Government man, I have not always been blind to the tubs that the ostriches in office throw to the whales; and the courteous reader I am sure will think with me, that it was a very doubtful regulation that deprived Custom-house officers and consuls of their fees. Indeed, I have always thought that the latter should have no salaries at all, but be paid by fees from those whose business they do; but let their fees be strictly regulated. It is a very hard thing for an old wife, in the wilds of Inverness-shire, to be paying in the price of her tea for consuls on the back of the world, whose only business is with men and matters that neither directly nor indirectly can she have any thing to do with.

But I am falling into an overly digression on this head; for I only meant to set forth that true national representatives, members such as I was, should in all alterations, even in things deemed corrupt, see in what manner the change has been beneficial to the public. Clear to me it is, that it was not the abolition of fees that was required, but only their regulation; and whoever was the father of that job, though it was one of the artificers of a new ministry, to curry favour with popularity, it was but a weak invention, and shewed no right conception of the business of the commercial world.

But it is time I should resume my narrative; for, although this explanation may in some degree be necessary to explain my conduct, I do not profess here to state my principles in any direct form. My object is to shew by my actions what they were, and it will be seen they continued as pure and independent after I became more of a politician than I was or intended to be in my early career. When I say this, I beg to be understood as in no sense implying that I gave much heed to international affairs; it would have been indeed an extraordinary departure from the consistency of my character, had I done so; for on that subject there are always between both sides of the house something less than a hundred members who are well qualified to keep their friends right. My endeavour, therefore, was not so much to acquire superior knowledge myself, as to acquiesce judiciously in the opinions of those who were best informed. And in this respect I was not singular in those days; for many sound and solid-headed elderly gentlemen, who did not know, when they entered the house, whether Portugal was in the kingdom of Lisbon, or Lisbon in the kingdom of Portugal, did the same thing, and their votes were always highly approved; for it so happened that they pinned their faith, like me, to the opinions of men that the general world out of doors respected for their talents, knowledge, and integrity.

CHAPTER XXV

Although the first session of my third parliament worked on myself a considerable change, and led me on to be more of a public and party man than was in exact conformity with my own notions of what a plain member should be, who has the real good of his country at heart, I yet had some small business in my own particular line; the most remarkable piece of which was in being balloted a member of a committee to try the election for the borough of Wordam, in which it was said that some of the most abominable bribery practices had taken place that ever offended the sight of the sun at noon-day. In this affair my old adversary at Frailtown, Mr Gabblon, was the sitting member; and to be sure the petitioners alleged against him such things as might have made the hair on the Speaker's wig stand on end 'like quills upon the fretful porcupine,' had they not been so well accustomed to accusations of the same kind.

It is true that there are few tribunals more pure and impartial than the election committees of the House of Commons; but incidents will occur in the course of an inquiry that are very apt to make the proceedings seem questionable; and thus it came to pass, that as we reported Mr Gabblon not duly elected, I suffered in the opinion of his friends, as having been swayed by the recollection of the trouble he had given me at Frailtown. No man, however, could act with stricter justice than I did: one of the committee, indeed, a new young member, fresh from Oxford, and aspiring for renown, said openly, that I had shewn a conduct throughout the investigation worthy of Rhadamanthus; which nick-name, by the by, did not stick to me, but to himself.

Among other charges, it was alleged against Mr Gabblon that he had hired a mountebank doctor and a merry-andrew to seduce the burgesses; I pricked up my ears at this, and looking from under my brows, and over the table to where the honourable gentleman was sitting, gave him, in spite of myself, a most, as he called it, taunting smile. Now, the truth was, that I only happened to call to mind what Mr Tough, my solicitor, had done with Doctor Muckledose at the Frailtown election. The mention of the mountebank did not, however, make a deep impression on the committee; indeed, some of themselves, if all tales be true, were well accustomed to such antics; but an answer to a very small question, which I put to one of the witnesses, threw great light on the subject.

'Friend,' quo' I to him, resting my arms and elbows on the table, and my chin upon the back of my hands, – 'did your mock-doctor vend medicines?'

'Oh, yes!' said the man; 'he had pill-boxes and salves.'

'And nothing else?' said I, seeing him hesitate.

'There was a wrapped-up paper.'

'Ay; and what was in it?'

'It was a printed note, saying that the doctor would be consulted by the freemen and their families gratis, every day till the election was over.'

'This looks serious!' exclaimed my Rhadamanthian friend; and I thereupon said to the witness, – 'And what was the result?'

'All,' quo' he, 'that consulted the doctor, it was said, were inoculated.'

'What do you mean by inoculated?'

'At the election they all voted for Mr Gabblon.'

'Well, my friend, but what had Mr Gabblon to do with that?' and, on saying this, I turned round to the chairman and said, 'The doctor and the merry-andrew should be called before us as witnesses.'

Upon which Mr Gabblon's lawyer objected, saying, 'They could not be legal witnesses, inasmuch as they were rogues and vagabonds by law.'

This was, however, overruled; and I saw Mr Gabblon turn of a pallid hue when it was determined to bring them before us.

We then adjourned to afford time, and in due season met again. The doctor and his fool were really very decent, just as respectable to look at as any member of the committee: the merry-andrew was dressed in the tip-top of the fashion, with an eye-glass, hung by a garter-blue riband. But what surprised me most was, that I was some time of discerning in him the same young man that had been so serviceable to Mr Tough at my own election.

As it was evident to the meanest capacity in the committee, that the inoculation had been performed by matter obtained from Mr Gabblon, I made a dead set at that point, and said to the clown in a conversible manner:

'And so, my old friend, for I see you are such, we have rather a knotty business in hand: what said the doctor, your master, to you

84

when he mentioned that you were hired to play your pranks for the edification of the good people of Wordam, as you were once hired by a friend of mine to do for me at Frailtown?'

'He said,' replied the young man very becomingly, 'that I should have five guineas.'

'Well, considering your talent, that was moderate; but I don't think you have improved in prudence since we met; for, according to report, you had as much from my friend for one day as for all the seven you performed for Mr Gabblon.'

'But, sir,' replied the witness, nettled at the idea of his prudence being called in question, 'I had five guineas every day.'

'Oh! I thought you only performed one day.'

'Yes, sir, only one day in public; but the private practice was no easy job.'

'No doubt,' said I; 'but what was this private practice?'

'It was bamboozling the natives before some of them were in a condition to take the doctor's drugs.'

'That was hard work, no doubt; but what was the doctor's medicine that the patients were so loath to take? To be sure drugs are very odious things.'

'I never saw him administer any.'

'You're a clever lad,' said I, 'and you'll just step aside and let the doctor come forward'; which being accordingly done, I continued:

'Doctor,' quo' I, 'I hope you're very well, and have been this long time; you keep your looks very well: no doubt you take a good deal of the same physic that your young man has been telling us was administered, *pro bono publico* and Mr Gabblon, at Wordam.'

'Not so much as I could wish,' replied the doctor; 'times are very hard.'

'No doubt they are; but what were the doses that operated so efficaciously at Wordam?'

'The Melham bank,' replied the doctor, 'had stopped payment.'

'Hey!'

Mr Gabblon gave a deep despairing sigh, and I said,

'Doctor, not to trouble you with these trifling questions, for I am sure your medicine was as precious as gold——'

'It was all sovereigns, for the cause I mentioned.'

Mr Gabblon gave another sigh, and his lawyer, albeit of a rosy hue, turned for a moment white as his wig, and then laughed.

'Doctor,' was my comment, 'we are very much obliged to you; your

85

answers have been exceedingly satisfactory: but one point; it's of no consequence; you should however have mentioned it; and that is, how you got the sovereigns.'

'Oh! Mr Gabblon's groom brought them every morning, and staid with me as long as patients came.'

'I daresay, doctor, you had many doubtful cases – what was the prevailing complaint?'

At these words, Mr Gabblon, not the wisest of mankind, suddenly started up, and called the doctor an ass, not to see how I was making a fool of him.

''Tis you,' said the clown, 'that he's making a fool of'; at the same time winking to the Committee with one of his stage faces, forgetful where he was.

In short, not to lengthen my story into tediousness, bribery and corruption was clearly proven; and Mr Gabblon, as I have already stated, was set aside; for he was not cunning enough, in a parliamentary sense, to be honest, – a thing which leads me to make an observation here, namely, that it is by no means plain why paying for an individual vote should be so much more heinous than paying for a whole borough.

CHAPTER XXVI

My third parliament was more remarkable for talk than trade. A great many motions were vehemently discussed, not one of which was of the slightest benefit to the nation. Those in the two early sessions were altogether what my friend Colonel Armor called 'drilling recruits', – that is, affording opportunities for young orators to shew the calibre of their understandings and the weight of their knowledge; and yet the sittings were busy and bustling to public members, and to the newspapers, for they filled their columns. For my part, I was sick of it; and a very little of the drug that the doctor distributed at Wordam would have made me retire to my cool sequestered neuk in Scotland, even though there is something in the air of the Parliament House that does wile a man on, from day to day, to thole with a great deal of clishmaclavars, – at least so it proved with me.

One advantage I derived by giving more ear to politics than in the two former Parliaments, – I was less troubled by applications for places, which are really very vexatious. As an independent member, applicants to me were both Whigs and Tories, – neither, to be sure, of a deep dye, but still party men; but when I began to adhere to the one party, I was none troubled by those of the other, it being an understood thing that I would only attend to applications from my brethren in feeling and principle. This I did not dislike to perceive and to know.

My own nature, and a rightful regard towards the Government, made me of a Toryish inclination, which I soon saw was the prevalent inclination of the House. By far the greatest part of the members were disposed to stand by the Government in all things, though there were schisms of a personal kind that it was fitting John Bull should not discern. These, accordingly, were ascribed to principles; but were, in fact, personalities which governed the selection of men for power and office.

By the best of my calculations the number of real Tories in the House never reached sixty persons; that is to say, sixty who would on no account listen to the slightest proposal for any alteration in the frame of our constitution and the ancient establishments, which they called its bodily organisation: they would have as soon listened to a proposition to change the physical position of the kingdom itself on the globe, as to change the relative position of the orders and institutions which time, and the frame of our government, had established; and which they thought were things that came as much of nature as the oak, or any other indigenous product. These I looked upon as the pillars of the state; but I was not myself one of them: on the contrary, I was more in conformity with the greater number, who thought that if a diseased limb was incurable it ought to be cut off, to preserve the health and strength of the whole body.

With the exception of the sixty unchangeable Tories, there was undoubtedly a disposition in all the rest of the House to encourage Government to persevere in a course of amendment, even to a recasting of the most consecrated usages and establishments of our ancestors. Among these were included, at this time, fully more than sixty Whigs; that is to say, men dissatisfied with the whole frame of existing things, and who thought that the world would be mended were that frame entirely removed, and a new system substituted.

Much did I meditate on the curious fact of the seeming equality in numbers between the inveterates of both sides of the House, or, rather, on the predominance which the Whigs appeared really to possess, without being themselves aware of it, till I began to institute a comparison of their respective individual qualifications; in which comparison the Tories, alike in talent, experience, and practical sense, so bore away the bell, that I soon ceased to wonder at their superiority of influence. Taking the numbers of deadly Whigs and Tories to be equal, I persuaded myself that, in point of those qualities which rule mankind, one Tory was equal to two Whigs; and that luckily for the nation it was so, otherwise we should have had nothing but changes, until not a stool was left to sit upon. It was merely in practical talent, however, that the Tories had the advantage – certainly not in numbers; for the House, in general, bent toward that course of action which the Whigs recommended. Throughout the whole of that parliament, a practical man among the Whigs was only wanting to have made them the masters.

Among other ineffectual controversies which arose out of the otherwise unproductive results of this debating Parliament, was what may be called the Money Question – a subject on which mercantile opinion is alone deserving of attention, but which has not been attended to throughout. The question concerning it, instead of relating to the thing itself, turned chiefly on the material of which the thing is made, the country gentlemen insisting that the money should be money's worth:

thus, that Government should always keep a vast sum, in the value of the material of tokens, circulating from hand to hand throughout the kingdom.

I was grievously puzzled in this matter, for some of those to whose opinions I pinned my faith in abstruse matters of policy, had really what seemed to me very wild notions on this subject. This arose from the theory being so different from the practice, as in many other things of Government; for certainly nothing can be plainer than that a bank-note, valid for its value, is as good as gold: and yet, notwithstanding the great cost of gold, the country gentlemen insisted that many millions' worth of it should be kept in circulation, and paper put down. The reason of their opinion, however, never appeared in the debates; they knew that the craft and fraudulency of the world would substitute an unsound paper, and that those who issued it would draw the gold into their own coffers. It was this craft and fraudulency that were dreaded, when the cry was got up that paper should be put down; and thus it happens, that the appearance of gold for bank-notes is a lasting testimony against the integrity of those bankers who then issued notes.

But my ultimate opinion on the subject was, that Government should have taken the matter into their own hands, and never have parted with the privilege of coining; for I could not discover that there was any difference, in the principle of coining, between stamping with a copper-plate on paper and with a die on gold.

As there was a frequent cry of money being scarcer at one time than another, I thought there must be some capricious operation at the ventricle from which it flowed. Accordingly, my conclusion was, that much of our embarrassment in money matters came from the Bank being allowed to vary in the amount of its issues; and it appeared to me, that in permitting this discretion in the Bank, sufficient considera-tion was never given to the power it had of extending or contracting its issues; or, in other words, of enlarging or diminishing the amount of its discounts.

But while I thought so, I was not so obstinate in my opinion as to be very pugnacious; therefore, in all the arguments concerning the Money Question, I uniformly paired off. I never heard such fulness of wisdom on the one side as to contradict the theories of the other. But in this matter I stood not alone; nor will I allow that it was a question which had any thing to do with the principles of Government, though it has been much made use of as such.

CHAPTER XXVII

But although in this Parliament I was, as I have stated, spared, in a measure, from the distress of many applications, compared to what I had been previously doomed to endure, yet I was not altogether spared; and one of the few – but these were enough – that gave me trouble, was rather more of a private than of a parliamentary nature.

I have had occasion to mention a Mr Selby, and how, in my opinion, he was not used well by the administration of the Government towards him. There might be faults on both sides, if things so unequal as a single subject and a Government can be supposed to stand in such relative comparison; but, as it seemed in his case, I must say, as a Government man, the chief fault lay on our side, and I will always think so; for the war was waged between two unequal adversaries – if war it can be called – the attacks of which, on the one side, consisted only of earnest and humble petitions.

One night, after a very jangling debate, of which I could make neither head nor tail, and came away from sheer weariness of spirit before it was ended, as I was leisurely picking my steps along the plain stones up Palace Yard, the Abbey clock boomed twelve. It was a starry night; the sounds and buzz of the far-spreading city around were sunk into a murmur, as soft as the calm flowing tide on the sands of the seashore; – it was a beautiful night, and the moon rode high and clear; not a breath was stirring, and the watchman, with his cry of 'past twelve o'clock', seemed as suitable to the occasion as the drowsy effigy of a dream going towards a weary politician's pillow.

I thought, coming out of the foul air of the close House, that I had never seen such a serene sweet night since I had left the cool and hallowed shores of the Ganges: a new sense, as it were, was opened in my bosom, like the fresh spring which Moses drew from the rock in the desert; and I said to myself, if I am becoming an older man, surely it is also pleasing Heaven to make me a better: and yet I was never much of a saint, though, in a parliamentary sense, I had an inclination for the pastures of these innocent and pawky creatures.

Stepping thus along with easy paces towards my lodgings in Manchester Buildings, as I passed the steps from Cannon Row to the back way that leads to the bridge, I beheld, by the glimpses of the moon, a remarkable young woman sitting there, with several children about her.

At such an hour and time, this was a sight that would have interested any man; and it found me in the season of my softness.

'Young woman,' said I, 'what are you doing at this time of night, with these children, sitting in such a melancholy posture, and in such an out-of-the-way place?'

Her head, at the time, was resting on her knees, and her face was pale and shining, like the moon in the heavens.

'We are,' replied she, 'waiting.'

'This is,' quo' I, 'a strange place to wait. For whom are you waiting?'

She looked up again, and all the children did so likewise, and then she said, 'For death!' and stooped down again, as if she cared not what I thought of her sad answer; but all the children gave a very pitiful wail.

Really, thought I, this is a strange scene to happen to a member coming from a debate for the good of the nation; and I was greatly rebuked and confounded.

'My good young woman,' said I, in amazement, 'what has put it into your head to make me such a reply?'

She looked up suddenly again for a moment, and said, 'Want.'

'Want! my leddy, what do you want?'

'Every thing, – parents, shelter, food, clothing, friends, – every thing that makes the curse or blessing of life.'

This was said as one that was well educated, and it put me in a most disordered state; I could therefore do no less than exclaim, 'My God! what are you to do?'

At which she started up on her feet and said, with a stern voice, 'To die!'

The other children at this began to cry, and she turned round and chided them, and then said to me,

'Sir, we are a family in utter misery. I have told you our condition – we are starving: can you help us? will you? if not, go away, and disturb us not while we perish.'

I was astonished, for she was but young in her teens, though she spoke as dreadful as a matron in years. What could I do but relieve their immediate grief with what small change I happened to have in my pocket? and I told her to take the children with her to where they had been sheltered the night before, and come to me in the morning and tell me her story. So I gave her my address, and bade her only to make haste to a refuge with her small sisters, and then bade them good night.

I can never think of that mournful adventure without a gruing of grief; for although nocturnal sights of unsheltered folk are not rare in Bengal, there is a mercifulness in the temperate air that mitigates the tooth of misery. Mankind suffer less, although their afflictions be equal, when the climate withholds the anguish of the cold that exasperates disease and starvation.

CHAPTER XXVIII

I did not pass that night with agreeable dreams, and I rose betimes for breakfast, with the discomfort of one that had suffered unrest. I had no relish, in fact, for the meal, and my Findhorn haddock was sent away untasted.

Just as the table was cleared, and my writing-desk placed before me, the young woman was announced; and having desired her to be shewn into the room, I prepared myself to hear a very deplorable story. I had not, however, inquired more than her name, which was Mary Selby, when a deputation from the country, of three gentlemen, was announced, respecting a new canal; I was thereupon obliged to request Mary Selby to retire for a little time, telling her I would see her when the deputation was gone. Accordingly, she rose to go out just as the gentlemen came in, and I observed, as she passed them, that she looked with a very remarkable expression of countenance at one of them, an elderly man with thin haffits and a bald forehead, but said nothing.

This deputation was from a part of the country of which I had no knowledge, and in which neither friend nor acquaintance; but their spokesman said to me, that they were under an obligation to intrude in consequence of the great power that was exerted against them.

I replied, 'that they were very right in the step they had taken; for I could not see that any reason existed why a member should not be canvassed for his vote and interest, in turn, as well as either a pot-walloper or freeholder, or any other of the elective gender;' at the same time remarking, however, 'that they ought to have a clear explanation of their case, for ordinarily, on private bills, this was too little attended to, the friends of the parties trusting chiefly to the votes they could muster; and thus it came to pass, from less to more, that we fell into a discourse concerning some of the usages of Parliament, and the inattention of Government to private bills, as if speculations that altered the interests and face of the country were things of no account.'

Some of the remarks made by the gentlemen on this head appeared to me at the time very striking, and have continued to stick by me since,

93

particularly those of the old man, at whom the young woman gazed with surprise and wonder. He was, indeed, a shrewd, solid, observing gentleman; and one of his sayings I shall never forget.

'In truth,' said he, 'it is a great defect in our Government, that the plans of public improvement are left entirely at the discretion of their projectors, who, if they be plausible persons, soon find support enough, by which works are undertaken that supersede others of more utility, and yet afterwards prove great losses. No private bill, for improvements of any sort, should be allowed to go before the House of Commons until the importance of the improvement proposed has been certified by a board or department of Government.'

I said to him 'that he was very right; but it was thought that these things were best left to the freedom and discretion of those who were interested in them.'

'I would, perhaps,' said he, 'leave a good deal to that opinion; but if the business of government be the protection of property, and I can see but little use for it besides, surely it is a blameable negligence to let the nation grow rife with public projects without investigating their utility.'

Soon after, the deputation went away; but, in leaving the room, something appeared to me in the behaviour of the old gentleman that shewed, as I thought, a disposition on his part to hold a private conversation with me. Accordingly, I said that every morning I would be found at home about the same hour, and if any of them had aught to say to me I would be glad to see them.

I then desired the servant to shew in the young woman, for I was fashed about her; but James replied to me that she was a strange behaved girl; 'for,' said he, 'though she is a beggar in rags, she's as proud as Lucifer, and would rather stand in the passage than come down stairs.'

'Very well, James,' quo' I, 'I'll look at that, and ye'll just send her in.'

Accordingly, in she came; but, instead of the sedate sadness of her former demeanour, I was surprised to see her weeping very bitterly, and yet with an air about her by common, insomuch that I was in a manner constrained to say, – 'My good girl, you see, business must be attended to; and it was not for disrespect to you that I gave a preference to the gentlemen.'

'I am well aware of that,' she replied; 'but in one of the gentlemen I discovered an uncle, who could never imagine that I or my mother's family were in such distress. Thank Heaven! I have been endowed with fortitude enough to conceal myself from him in the presence of those he was with.'

This news startled me exceedingly; and her name recalling to my recollection that of the gentleman for whom I had been formerly so interested with Government, I inquired if she knew any thing of him.

'Yes; he was my father,' was the reply. 'He is dead, and my mother is dead, and every thing she left is gone and sold; and last night, had you not pitied us, perhaps we had been this morning all no more: but the sight of my uncle has revived my hope, and the despair that was at my heart begins to relent.'

'Why did you not seek out your uncle?'

'We had not time, distress came upon us so rapidly; nor did we well know where to find him.'

After some further discourse, I agreed to get her uncle's address in town, which was done that same forenoon; and he behaved towards her like a worthy man, taking her and her sisters under his care with a sympathising heart. Two striplings that were younger than her, and older than the little girls, had gone upon the world to provide for themselves, and some days elapsed before they were found. At last they were rescued, and the whole family were removed into the country.

It was in the course of this transaction that he explained to me what he was moved to say privately to myself on our first interview; and this was to tell me, that he had heard his unfortunate brother mention my name warmly, as one of the very few about the House of Parliament that would listen long enough to understand his grievous and peculiar case.

This I was both proud and sorry to hear, because, to give the devil his due, there is not any wilful shutting of the ear about a member of Parliament on either side; and it only requires a reason and method in applying to them to get their good will, if the matter you trouble them with will bear sifting. So that out of this small adventure, painful as it was, I reaped some good fruit, for, besides the complacency which I enjoyed at hearing how well pleased a most unfortunate man was with me in a very cruel predicament, I had the satisfaction to discern that the course I pursued, of listening with patience even to strangers on private bills, was judicious, and in salutary accordance with what the Government naturally expects from members of the private and domestic kind.

CHAPTER XXIX

The do-little Parliament, as I have always considered that third one to have been with respect to the nation, was however of some effect to myself, inasmuch as in the course of it, growing something more of a politician than previously, my attention was directed to divers things of consequence, which at first I did not perceive: as such, not the least of these was our foreign affairs and the Holy Alliance: the latter subject, I never thought was rightly considered among us.

We regarded that conjunction of monarchs in too special a manner, as I thought; for somehow we took it into our heads that it was an alliance of sovereigns against subjects; whereas, if we had regarded it as an alliance for the upholding of governments as they are, with respect to one another, it would have drawn us to a wiser conclusion.

Before it was contrived governments had no tribunal of appeal against the aggressions of each other, but only arms; and this, in the existing state of knowledge, was but a poor and barbarous alternative. There was, however, no reason why the community of governments or of kings should remain in this base condition; and whatever therefore the artifices and craft of diplomaticians may have turned the Alliance to, there was, undoubtedly, something wise and grand in the first conception, of making the nations of the world responsible to an earthly tribunal, like individuals in private life to the courts of law.

No doubt the French revolution had caused the governments of the world to look with apprehension on the internal movements of nations; but there was a wide difference between upholding an established government, and denying to it the power and privilege of conceding the reforms which its people demanded. This distinction, however, I for one thought our politicians never very accurately made; at least, I never could exactly see that the Holy Alliance, which took upon itself only the preservation of peace, presumed to meddle with the internal affairs of nations, until the existing government was in danger of overthrow, and was unable to maintain itself.

This notion of mine was not, however, very general among my friends, but I have ever abided by it; and will to the last of my days remain persuaded, come what may, that it was a great improvement in the international system of the world to make governments responsible to one another. War, as we all have seen and experienced, is a dreadful alternative, and too much of the machinery of nations is contrived to render it at all times easily undertaken; as if the warlike strength of a state constituted its chiefest glory.

But as I am not writing political disquisitions, I may as well no further advert to the subject here, than to observe an effect which the Alliance had among us, leading to considerations that at one time it would have been thought very strange to have entertained.

Without being aware of the tendency of what they said, those politicians who have cried out so lustily against the principle of the Holy Alliance, now see a very bad effect of their conduct fast coming to a head. They have sown distrust between subjects and governments – by their arguments endeavouring to shew that the governors have interests apart from the governed; and this has weakened their reciprocal ties to such a degree, that even the foundations of property, the oldest and most consecrated of temporal things, are now in a state of being moved: the result who can tell? In a word, a wild and growing notion prevails that governments, and all things pertaining to them, are of less use than had been always supposed; a doctrine which, in the struggle of asserting, the most civilised and refined communities will be driven to the wall.

Before the time of this Parliament, according to my reflections, the kingly portion of the state was considered a thing necessary and indestructible, and whose utility it was denying first principles to call in question; but, from some of the discussions alluded to, it has ceased to be an undisputed thing, whether in England there should be a monarchy, or any other principle of government acknowledged than the opinion of the present age. By and by we shall see that this notion has been extending itself, and that, in consequence, many of those things which made the grandeur of England, have been, by the unconscious invidia of those whose lot in life makes them of the lower orders, deteriorated not only in veneration but utility.

However, it is of no consequence now to state my opinion of the Holy Alliance, nor to lament that so little use was made at the time of the magnanimity in which it was conceived. It was received in a mean and distrustful spirit by the radical politicians, and it was no more than natural that the authors should resent to the utmost the ill-humour with which their gracious intentions were even in this country repelled. In the House of Commons, I very well recollect, that not a few decent, gash, and elderly carles laughed, forsooth, at the pious terms in which the objects of the Alliance were expressed, and also a number of the juvenile Machiavelli that infest the benches saw nothing in it but the raw-heads and bloody-bones of bastiles and tyranny. It is no doubt true that the Holy Alliance had not been long promulgated, till several of its members drew back in the performance of promises which they had made in times of peril to their people; but little heed has been given to the cause – the fact only has been recollected. Now, although I am free to confess, as we say in Parliament, that this is a black fact, still I am not so thoroughly versed in continental politics as to be able to give it a downright condemnation, because we soon saw, that what was called the peace of Europe was but as ice upon the surface of a lake, that was liable to be tossed by a storm. In no other respect, but as the outbreakings of a deep and wide-spread disease, have I ever been able to look on those Carbonari, and other discontented eruptions, which, from time to time, took place; and which served to shew that the right-ful season for changes in the old establishments of the governments of Europe had not come to pass. There was not that sane and wholesome understanding existing between rulers and people, without which the attempt to improve is always dangerous. And in consequence, for the life of me, as an honest man, I never could see that the kings and princes who promised constitutional governments were to blame for with-holding them, merely from feeling their hands strengthened by joining themselves together in an equitable league.

CHAPTER XXX

Many things in the midst of the do-little disputations indicated to older members that a change of some kind was coming over the British Government; and it was pointed out to me, by the late Sir Everard Stubble, that there was more passion and less firmness in the tone of public men towards one another than he recollected in better times. He was one of the stanch Tories, and, probably, on that account more sensitive to mutations than me; at least so it happened, that although he felt the chilness of a coming shadow – the shadow of change, and spoke of it as a certainty, he yet could not point out the reasons of his belief.

I saw, however, that men spoke to one another with less severity about reform, and anent Catholic emancipation, than they had done in times bygone; indeed, many of the lighter-minded, who look to a division of the House of Commons as the settling of a question, expressed a wish that the latter business was determined, seeing that sooner or later it must be given up. To say the truth, I was not myself, as an independent member, far from that opinion; for when I considered that a matter was so ripened by many discussions as to carry the minds of the majority out of doors, it was no longer prudent to let it be delayed.

But I cannot say, that in acceding to this notion my judgment just entirely approved the expediency of granting full relief to the Catholics; for I could not shut my eyes to the historical truth, that the church endowments had once been theirs, and that their priesthood had as good a right, from that circumstance, to share, in proportion to their numbers, the loaves and the fishes with our own, both on this side of the water and in Ireland. Thus, though in the subsequent Parliament I did give my vote for the Catholic Relief Bill, still I have never ceased to fear that I thereby assisted to open a door for the admission of new troubles. But while I say this, I would not retract that vote, unless there was a clear visibility that the human mind was going backward. It was, however, a vote in obedience to the signs of the times; and I have never ceased to lament the night on which public duty, rather than private judgment, compelled me to give it.

Had the great sacrifice which was then made of the constitution of

1688 been followed by the requisite measure of equalising, according to their numbers, the claims of the Catholics and the Protestants on the property of the church, I would have submitted with more contentment, even although in doing so the pretensions of Dissenters to a share of that property had been considered. But when I saw nothing of the kind done, I began to be afraid; for in making Catholics no better than Dissenters, we were stirring up anew an enemy that it had taken both time and trouble to lay; and it only saddens my heart and deepens my sorrow for the vote I gave, seeing that it has been followed by no proposition to redress the grievance which the necessity of giving it implied.

The more I reflect on this measure, wise in its object, but abortive in the hopes it promised, the more am I satisfied, that the great predominant party in the State, which had so long held the reins of government, was at the end of its stage. I could discern that there was not, as formerly, that true stubborn adherence to Government which characterised its old supporters; and that there was, in fact, many among them with anchor a-trip, ready to join the other squadron. Altogether, my reflections on the Catholic emancipation gave me no pleasure: not that I find fault with the measure itself, for that was carried in a high and masterly manner; but because, after it was done, nothing else followed, but only those evils which the adversaries of granting the relief predicated – evils which are full rapidly kithing. But to return. Although the issue of the Catholic question was seen to be inevitable, during the Parliament that I will never cease to describe as the do-little, other things that greatly shattered the consistency of the Tories.

From time out of mind there had been certain rules and laws for the regulation of shipping and commerce, which we, of our party, had all along maintained were essential to the support of our national superiority. They were made expressly for that object; and the greatest talents which our statesmen ever displayed, were exerted in vindicating those ancient national measures. It was, therefore, a dreadful shock to our affections when we heard the merits of them condemned. I am really not sure that this did not do more to dissolve the Tory adherency than even that laxity of constitutional principle which afterwards led to the measure of the Catholic Relief Bill.

No doubt, in the abstract, there was much truth in the reasons urged for the alteration, considering the facility which the then state of the world afforded; but the difference of condition between us and foreign countries was not considered with that fulness it ought to have been. Theoretical principle was more consulted than practice, and the result was, at least to many of us, doubtful. I therefore look upon the free-trade doctrine, and the doctrine upon which the Catholic relief was founded, viz. that all mankind had natural rights in society, as truths of the same science, but as such liable to be regulated by expediency.

In all this it was plain to me, as well as to others, that the Whig party was strengthened in the House, by an accession of those who called themselves Liberals going over from our side to them, not in a palpable body; and that the Tories were losing strength and numbers. A third party, mongrel Whigs, was forming.

This state of things was very puzzling to me, especially as the retrenchment, of which old Sir John Bulky had given me notice, was duly lopping off the means that I had looked to for my share of patronage – one of the principal inducements which led me originally to think it advisable to go into Parliament. In short, it seemed to me that Government was unconsciously weakening itself on all hands, and that the lofty pile of our monarchy was sustaining, by our contempt for old experience, and the substitution of new theories for ancient customs, some detriment, that might go hard in time with its very existence.

CHAPTER XXXI

The corn-laws, although it cannot be said that any new light has been thrown upon them in the course of my parliamentary life, have yet occupied no small share, during it, both of public and of private attention. Respecting them I never have considered myself as very competent to judge; for when I bought my estate of the Girlands, I knew that I had paid for it what is called a high war-price, and that it was only by future improvements I could ever expect to make it a profitable investment; in so far, therefore, I could take a free and common-sense view of the matter.

The ordinary argument among the country gentlemen, as it struck me, was, that the produce of the soil was as justly entitled to protection as the produce of the loom, or any other manufacture. This seemed a very fair statement; for if we prohibited, in any degree, by duties or regulations, the importation of raiment, and articles of that sort, there could be no injustice in doing as much towards food, which was not more necessary.

The operatives, however, who, without disparagement, may be said to cherish a selfish feeling on every question in which their own interests are concerned, have uniformly taken a very different view of the subject. Nothing would, to them, be more satisfactory than an entire prohibition of all foreign articles similar to those of their own manipulation; yet they cry out, as if they were the victims of gross legislative partiality, at every step which the farmer takes to insure a protecting price for the produce of the soil and his labour.

The question, stated thus, seems reasonable, and ought to lead both parties to a right understanding; but it does not do so, and there does exist, in consequence, a very unfair and unjust opinion among the operatives against the agricultural interest.

How the difference between them is ever to be reconciled, is a knotty point of policy, and much have I reflected upon the subject, evening and morning, and midtime of day – yea, even in the watches of the night. But the o'ercome of my meditations has ever been, that the spirit of the times runs strong and unjustly against the lords and traders whose business is with the soil; and the conclusion to which I have come is now a part of my parliamentary creed, namely, that a judicious legislature should only endeavour to regulate the trade in corn, and that the abolition of the laws against the importation of foreign corn should be according to the traffic which foreign countries hold with us for our manufactures.

A plan of this sort, however, will not satisfy the operatives, who, in their one-eyed view of commerce, imagine that a different law should regulate the trade in earth or grain from that which regulates it in silk or cotton: and upon this subject I have had several solid conversations with friends and neighbours – merchants, manufacturers, and country gentlemen – without acquiring much instruction from them.

It appears to me that there is a disposition of a general kind existing in the public, to regard the produce of the soil as something foreign from other descriptions of produce. The operatives think they have a right to exchange the productions of their art for things which they cannot produce; and that if they can find food cheaper by sending their articles for it abroad, they have a right to do so, and that nothing but a usurpation on the part of the country gentlemen prevents them. This is surely not sound, for the manufacturer – the collective representative of the operatives – cannot do without the merchant; and he it is who regulates the markets, and who considers corn a merchandise as much as any of the other stuffs and manufactures in which he deals.

Though it may serve the merchant's turn, were there no corn laws, to bring at times the cheaper corn of foreign countries into our markets, it behoves the operatives to consider by what means this is to be done. If he can bring, for a given quantity of their productions, a greater quantity of foreign corn than the same things would procure of home growth, then the argument of the operatives would so far be correct; but, if instead of sending our manufactures abroad to obtain corn in return, he is obliged to send money, look at what would be in the end the effect to the operatives? Would not the money thus sent be taken from the capital of the kingdom, and would not that capital so diminished lessen the means of employing the operatives, and thus bring round to them an evil as great as the difference of price between what they pay for corn brought in under regulations, and what they would pay were the trade free in that article.

But I will say no more on this head. All I intended by stating it was, to shew with what views I have been actuated in the different votes which I have given on this abstruse question. I cannot, however, restrain my indignant pen from noticing, with the strongest expressions of reprobation, those bad and ignorant men who go about the country stirring up strife and opposition between the two great interests into which the nation is naturally divided – the landed and manufacturing. It is to men of common understandings so plain that these interests are inseparable, that it seems scarcely inferior to a species of treason to make any sort of distinction between them; and yet how widely and wildly has this been done, and how strenuously have the malignant advocates of a free trade in corn deceived the operatives, and taught them, disastrously, to think, that a great, populous, and enlightened nation can have any reluctance to adapt its code of corn or of commercial law to any but right expedients?

CHAPTER XXXII

Whilst this change and enlargement of my mind was going on, his Majesty King George IV, that gorgeous dowager, departed this life; an event of a serious kind to me, and to those with whom I acted; for although our grief on the occasion was not of a very acute and lachrymose description, it was nevertheless heartfelt; for he stood in our opinion as the last of the regal kings, that old renowned race, who ruled with a will of their own, and were surrounded with worshippers.

'Never more,' said I, 'shall we have a monarch that will think his own will equivalent to law. His successors hereafter will only endeavour to think agreeably to their subjects; but the race of independent kings is gone for ever.' In a word, the tidings of his death, though for some time expected, really smote me as a sudden and extraordinary event. Had I heard that the lions had become extinct on the face of the earth, I could not have been more filled, for a season, with wonder and a kind of sorrow.

The most important upshot to myself, however, of this demise of the crown, was the dissolution of Parliament; for the King's illness had allowed time, if it had been made use of, to undermine my interest at Frailtown; but, by some strange cause, no effort of that kind was made. I and Lord Dilldam were hand and glove; for my politics, though I adhered to the Duke's party, were not greatly adverse to his lordship's; and the pruning of the Government patronage left but little on that score to differ about. I think it was owing to this cordiality between me and his lordship, that the election at Frailtown went off so smoothly; for, no doubt, had Lord Dilldam put his shoulder to the wheel against me, I would have had a heavy pull; for, to say the truth, his lordship was much beloved in that quarter; and although he was not a man that could be esteemed for talent, he was the best of masters and of landlords, and took sincere pleasure in putting himself on a pleasant footing with his tenantry and the inhabitants of the town. He was, indeed, one of those weak good men who so conduct themselves as to render the possession of great wisdom and ability of doubtful value.

I did not, however, in my own secret mind, relish the perfect smoothness with which I was returned for Frailtown. It seemed to me, that with a new king, and with such signs in the times as were then palpable, it was not a thing to be trusted, but, on the contrary, was very ominous, betokening rather an unripeness of purpose among the inhabitants than a party hesitation.

For some time it was well known that the growth of radicalism was spreading, and that the people were gone a degree beyond Whiggery in the malady. Now, I was a moderate Tory, that is to say, one who, when he saw repair or amendment necessary, would not object to the same, especially when the alteration was recommended by Government; and Lord Dilldam's politics were of the same colour, but a shade deeper. This I well knew, and could not but think that it was very odd how our united interests, which were so opposite to the conceits of the populace, were not resisted. And when I met his lordship in town, after the election, I spoke to him concerning the same.

'My Lord,' quo' I, 'what is your opinion of the lull that now prevails at Frailtown; I fear it augurs no good to your lordship's influence, and as little to the permanency of mine.'

'My dear Mr Jobbry,' was his answer, 'you never were more out in your conjectures. The good people of Frailtown do not see where they could find a better member than yourself; and having an idea that I am of the same opinion, which, without compliment, I frankly acknowledge, they are content to leave the care of their political interests in our hands.'

'I wish your lordship may be correct,' was my dubious reply; 'but, throughout the land, there is an unwholesome crave for something or another; and I have my apprehensions that Frailtown has not escaped the infection. In truth, my lord, I jalouse that the inhabitants are no longer content with the power of election remaining, under the old charter, in the corporation.'

'What reason,' said his lordship, after a pause of thoughtfulness, 'have you for that opinion? It is, however, not to me alarming,' he added; 'for though the elections were thrown open to the general burgesses, it would make but little difference, my family having been so long popular and well beloved among the inhabitants.'

I was very sorry to hear his lordship, worthy man! speaking in such delusion; but I had not the heart to break his dream of complacency. I saw, however, that my own reign in Frailtown was coming to a conclusion, notwithstanding the calm that then seemed to smile upon it. I therefore began to debate with myself, whether I ought not to dispose of my seat in a reasonable time; but the sort of attachment that I had taken to the House, and the rational amusement that was now and then to be obtained there, when discreet men spoke of the affairs of the nation, had its weight upon me, and I came to no determination.

There was, indeed, an interest arising from the state of the country that had its effect upon me; and I had a kind of a longing to wait till it would come to some result. This, no doubt, was partly owing to the stramash that had taken place at Paris, which had made the cocks and leaders of the radicals among ourselves crouse and bold. At the same time, I was not without a sense of apprehension concerning the Duke's government, his grace having declared himself so stubbornly devoted to the existing frame of our constitution. That speech I ever regarded as a declaration of war against the radicals; but I had such confidence in him, that while he found himself able to stand in the stronghold of office, I had no fear; still, I ought not to disguise the fact, that all things in the country, at the meeting of the new Parliament, looked in a very grievous condition; and I did not think the Duke stood upon a rock, – the more especially as his ministerial forces were not armed with weapons to contend with those who had gained the ears of the people against them, nor were they prepared with the measures requisite to quench the Irish kind of misrule that was raging in different parts of the kingdom. All things, indeed, had a very bad aspect; but still I was not so strongly minded to quit my public post, as perhaps a man of more prudence would have been. In this crisis I got a severe lesson.

CHAPTER XXXIII

One Friday night, or rather Saturday morning, after a husky debate, Mr Boldero Blount invited me to go down with him, next day, to his country seat. Says he to me, 'I have had a letter from my wife, telling me that she is very uneasy on account of the state which she hears the country is in; not that any thing has yet happened, but rumours are going about which make her very unhappy; so I have resolved to go down tomorrow, and to return on Tuesday; and would be glad if you would take a corner in my post-chaise, especially as no particular business is coming on.'

I accepted Mr Blount's offer; saying, at the same time, 'that I had heard very uncomfortable tidings from his part of the country; and nothing would give me more satisfaction than to see with my own eyes, and hear with my own ears, the truth and circumstance of the matters reported.

Accordingly, early in the afternoon we set off for his place, and arrived in time for a late but very excellent dinner; after which, to be sure, Mrs Blount gave us a sore account of the state of the laborous peasantry in the neighbourhood.

'They have not,' said she, 'broken out into any outrage as yet; but they hold meetings in bands in the evening, and think the scarcity of work is all owing to the tithes and the high rents, which their employers the farmers pay, in addition to their share of the taxes.'

This, as it seemed, was a brief and clear account of the discontent; and we had all the servants about the house brought in one by one, and examined on the subject anent such particulars as they had severally heard.

When this was done, Mr Blount, who was an off-hand man, and went at once to the marrow of most things, said,

'This notion of the peasantry is plainly a thing ingrafted upon them, and not of their own induction.'

I thought so too; but I said to him,

'It is, however, not the time now to inquire from what airt this wind comes, but to think of sheltering ourselves from the blast. Tomorrow is the Sabbath day; the country folks and farmers will be at the church:

let us both cast ourselves familiarly among them, and reason with them.'

The which Mr Blount most cordially approved of; and then, as we sat over our wine, we discoursed more anent the growth of the new doctrine concerning rent.

'It rises,' said Mr Blount, 'from that sound that has been echoing through the kingdom for a long time about the burden of our taxes.'

'No doubt of it,' replied I; 'but the weight of taxes is comparative with the means of payment, and there must be something very strange in the condition of our nation which makes us now, when we are relieved from the expenses of the war, less able than when under them to bear the public burdens.'

'That is the puzzle, Mr Jobbry: what can it be? for no truth can be more self-evident than that there has been a withdrawing from us of some secret thing that must have counteracted the burdens of the war. Have you any notion what it can be?'

'It can be no small matter, Mr Blount, since it is equivalent in effect to millions on millions on pounds sterling. In my opinion, it can have been no less than a great sum subtracted from the money among hands, or what the political economists call a contraction of the circulating medium.'

'By Jove!' cried Mr Blount, 'you have hit the nail on the head. The Bank has contracted its issues to a vast amount, equal to much of the reduced taxation; the country bankers are like shelled peascods, not a tithe in their notes to what they were: no bills are circulating for the munitions of war. Upon my word, Mr Jobbry, I do think that all our evils arise from our contracted circulation. But, although this be the root of the evil, what are we to do to get these crotchets out of the minds of the deluded commonalty?'

'That's a heavy question, and I fear cannot be answered, even by looking at those who have an interest in promoting the discontent.'

'Ay! who are these? not the poor, simple people, – they are but the instruments: for though tithes and taxes were all abolished tomorrow, they would get no more than their hire, and that hire would bring them no more than a subsistence. It is the rule of Providence and Nature that it should be so, and so it must continue until machinery comes to the head that the perfectibilians dream of, as to abridge in all things the labour of man.

'If it's not the common people,' quo' I, 'it cannot be the landlords, nor can it be the priesthood; for the rent of the one is not better founded than the tithes of the other. If the tithes were taken off, the landlord would increase his rent, and what would the public benefit by such a change?'

'That is not the radical doctrine,' replied Mr Blount: 'they don't want to take off the tithes altogether, but to apply them in mitigation of the taxes, and to let the churchmen make a living for themselves in the best manner they can.'

'It may be so, Mr Blount; but I doubt the country rioters do not consider the matter so finely. Now I'm going to say a harsh thing; but don't get angry if you differ from me.'

'Well, let's hear it.'

'You see, my good friend, that the farmers are the only parties that really could expect to profit by the abolition of tithes and the reduction of rents.'

'Surely, Mr Jobbry, you would not insinuate that the farmers are the authors of these outrages which so disgrace the country?'

'That is another question, Mr Blount; but I mean to say, that they are interested in propagating the opinions by which the labourers are misled; and we must not disguise it from ourselves, that there begins to be a very dangerous opinion hearkened to in the world, namely, that both landlords and an established priesthood are not necessary.'

'That notion is indeed very tremendous; it strikes at the root of property: no man under it could have any thing that he might call his own.'

'I do not, Mr Blount, at all think that the opinion is sound; but it is an opinion that is spreading abroad, – a disease, a moral cholera, if you please; but if all things are to be measured by utility, or, in other words, by their money value, what is to become of the world? In short, Mr Blount, it's my notion, that some of our cleverest men, and those too in the highest places, have been overly eager in propagating what may be called abstract theoretical truths; and that the modification which is requisite in practice to fit them for men's different humours and characters has been too little attended to. We want men who understand the tendency of the current to stem it boldly; for there is a hurry in the course of men's thoughts that cannot be checked too soon or too steadily.'

Just as we were thus speaking, Mrs Blount, who had for some time before retired, came flying into the room, saying that the light of three distant conflagrations was then visible, and that farmer Haselhurst's stack-yard was in flames, and a great crowd around it huzzaing and rioting.

This made us gather to our feet; but the particulars require another chapter.

CHAPTER XXXIV

The house of Elmpark, as the country-seat of Mr Boldero Blount was called, stood on a rising ground, and in daylight commanded a beautiful prospect down a long valley, in the bottom of which winded a broad and bright stream. Several villages, with trees and steeples, were seen on the sides of the valley, and far down the river was a mill with a bridge across; making a picture that was most delightful to contemplate in the morning or the evening, when the sun was shining. But on that night, when we sallied out in front of the house, it presented another sight. The darkness was clouded, and only a few stars could here and there be seen; but the distance was dismal. On the east, a wide and red glare was burning, – it cast no light in a manner upon any object, which made it very dreadful to behold; nearer, and in the south, there was another fire, the flames of which, licking the very clouds, could be distinctly seen, and black gables among them; and there was a window in one of the gables that shone like a star, but whether from a light within, or the reflection, nobody among us could tell. At a short distance from this great conflagration, we saw another farm-steading all in a blaze, which, although not so considerable, was yet very terrible to see; but the worst of all the spectacle was, the farm of Mr Haselhurst. It was less than two miles off, and the fire was very vehement: every thing in and about his farm-yard was distinct, and we saw the black figures of the crowd moving to and fro in terrible shapes around it. One of the mob I could clearly see, with my own eyes, whirling a cart-wheel into the midst of the burning, and Mrs Blount saw likewise another fling a ladder upon the flames. It was an awful sight.

Mr Blount was very calm and collected; and he said to his servants, and some labouring men that had come round the house, –

'Friends, these rioters will be here; but, if you are true men, they shall not burn us out both with ease and honour. Get ready the guns, and shut up the lower windows as well as you can, and prepare to receive them at those of the drawing-room floor.'

On his saying this, all the servants and labourers declared their readiness to defend the house; which, on hearing, I said to Mr Blount, 'that as I was a stranger and unknown, I would just walk down to Mr

112

Haselhurst's farm, and see what the mad criminals were really about, if there was any body that he could spare to shew me the road.'

To this proposition Mr Blount readily acceded; and, with one of his gardener's sons, a hobbletehoy of a laddie about fourteen, I walked towards the scene of destruction. I never, however, reached it; for when we were yet less than a quarter of a mile from the place, we met the crowd running and scattered, pursued by a whirlwind of dragoons, and a cloud of the county magistrates and gentlemen blowing at their heels.

Me and the laddie who was my guide stood up at a field-gate, to let the uproar pass, when, to my consternation, before I could open my mouth, a fat justice of the peace seized me, like a bull-dog, by the throat; and at the same time one of the dragoons struck the boy with the flat of his sword down into the ditch.

'Friends! in the name of peace and the king, what are you about? Unhand me!' cried I.

By this time the main body had ridden on, and I was left, with the poor greeting laddie, in the hands of the Philistines.

'Let me be,' said I to the fat magistrate; 'let us both be: we are innocent people.'

'We shall see to that,' cried a young man; and with that he caused a groom to come with a whip-cord and bind our hands behind our backs, in spite of all that I could say in remonstrance; and when I told my name, and that I was a Member of Parliament, they only tightened the cords, and caused me and my poor terrified guide to walk towards a turnpike-house, where they obliged us to mount into a cart. My heart was roasting with indignation; and the more I said to them the less would they hear. At last, we reached the borough-town, where they intended to put us in jail. The whole town was in commotion: women crying, and running dishevelled to and fro, and candles were at the windows.

When the cart stopped before the door of the Talbooth, seeing that no attention was paid to what I said to my conductors, I called quietly to a young man in the crowd hard by, and requested him to go to the mayor of the town, and tell him who I was, and that in their frenzy they had, by mistake, made a prisoner of me.

The young man was in the greatest consternation at hearing this: with nimble heels he went to the mayor; and presently a great hur got up, candles were brought, and much ado was made to lift me and the gardener's son out of the cart. But although everybody around said, any one without an eye in his head might have seen it was not probable that we were of the rioters, still the fat justice of the peace that took me so unmannerly and suddenly by the throat, maintained that I was only an imposter, and that I was no other than the old fellow Swing, that drove about the country in a gig with a gray horse, with combustibles, stirring the peasantry into rebellion.

Really, my corruption rose against that man; and if something had not restrained my arm, I would have cloven his skull with one of the council-room brass candlesticks; but a gentleman who was there pacified me, and said to the others that he would be responsible for the truth of my story. This served to moderate my wrath; but it was not till an express was sent for Mr Boldero Blount, and he was brought there present at the midnight hour, that they were satisfied.

It is very true that Mr Blount and me have many times since had a hearty laugh at the adventure: but I have often thought that the mistake with regard to me was a sample of real doings elsewhere; for I could observe, that more than one of the magistrates had but little command of his senses, and that even if I had been a guilty one, caught, as was thought, in the fact, there would have been no injustice in handling me with a little more consideration.

However, my case was but as a drop in the bucket compared with the calamities which began that night; and, to say the least, it would have been more creditable to the justices if, instead of watching till the nocturnal hours, and then scouring the country with dragoons before them wherever they saw a light, they had soberly, in daylight, set themselves in council, and considered the complaints of the people. My friend, Mr Blount, in his straightforward way, was an exception. He inquired into the matter, and even, where need was, gave help, though that was not often required; and, in consequence, both his own premises and his farms sustained no damage.

CHAPTER XXXV

In consequence of these terrible hobbleshaws we did not return to London so soon as we intended; for Mr Blount judiciously thought that the matter should be inquired into, and I thought the same thing. Accordingly, we spent several days on this business.

He caused the principal farmers around to be invited to his house, and several decent old gaffers from the neighbouring villages, together with a Mr Diphthong, who was a schoolmaster, well known in that part of the country to have much to say with the common people, being a young man of parts, and both for learning and capacity above many in his line.

These guests we sifted with a scrutinising spirit; and it was very lamentable to hear how far the judgment of some of them had gone astray: indeed, it is not saying too much to assert that, with the exception of Mr Diphthong, who really was a clever lad, scarcely one of them had a mouthful of common sense, the which made me jalouse that some of them were nigh at hand during the burnings.

However, though it was a task of some difficulty, we made out pretty plainly that the rioters were not instigated by want, which was most distressing to ascertain; for if they had, then there would have been some palliation for their mad conduct. Nor were they altogether set on by the spirit of revenge for wrongs or hardships they had sustained; but only out of a mistaken notion, that by so shewing themselves they would force on a reformation of the national abuses, as they considered them, not only in tithes and rents, but taxes and poor-rates. Against the latter, in particular, our informers said all the lower orders were just vicious.

It was not easy to see how a remedy could be applied to such a sweeping complaint. For my part, I was greatly dumbfoundered, and Mr Blount was no better; it being very manifest, that at the bottom of these opinions of the common people lay no less than a notion, that somehow, by the removal of oppressions, every labourer would live like a gentleman. Some, no doubt, knew better; and of them it may be said, that they only blew the coals to a certain degree, thereby hoping to achieve some mitigation of the public burdens.

One remark made by Mr Diphthong, however, on the poor-rates, struck both me and Mr Blount as very uncommon.

'Much,' said he, 'of this unhappy state of the country lies in a mere name; and were a little pains taken to place the matter in a proper light and ministration, a great deal of the discontent among the rural population would be appeased. There has grown up,' he continued, 'a disposition to consider all those as paupers who are employed by the parishes, as well as those who are assisted with alms by the parishes. This should be rectified.'

Mr Blount, evidently surprised to hear him say so, inquired what he meant.

'I mean,' was his reply, 'that the money raised to mend the parish roads, and to do other parish work, ought not to be included in the poor rates; for where the parish gets work done in return for employing the labourers when work is scarce, it ought not to be considered that the wages of these labourers are alms. It would be just as equitable to call the bricklayers who are now building the new church paupers, as those poor men who are breaking stones for the improvement of the highways. And thus it is that I say the error is in a name. Why not call the fund that is made use of for parish improvements the labour fund, and keep it distinct from the poor-rates? Were this done, certain am I, from what I have observed in our own parish, there would not be found any such increase of pauperism, as it has been of late years so much the fashion to enlarge upon. Indeed, I am so well convinced of this, that I do not believe the real poor-rates are at this time so great as they were at the beginning of King George the Third's reign, if the increase of population be considered – I mean the amount paid to the aged and infirm, for whom alone they are raised.'

'I doubt,' replied Mr Blount, 'you are making a distinction without a reason. It is employment that is wanted, and what signifies it whether the man that stands in need of employment be employed by the parish or gets alms.'

'A wide difference, Mr Blount. What the labourer gets for his labour is his own – he has earned it with the sweat of his brow – but alms are humbling; and no man likes to be an object of pity.'

I said, 'that I thought the observation very sensible; but still I did not very clearly see how to take work for alms differed from giving them for God's sake.'

'No?' replied Mr Diphthong: 'do not the paupers, to use an ignominious term, work on the roads to make them smoother? Compare the country roads of England with what they were only a few years ago, and say if the public has derived no advantage? Do not your waggons carry more and draw easier? And the same thing may be said of every transportable commodity. Is there no advantage in that?'

'Yes, Mr Diphthong,' replied Mr Blount, 'what you say is true. But were it not for the want of employment otherwise, we could do very well were our roads and hedges less trim.'

'Not so, sir: we are now a more refined nation than we were,' answered Mr Diphthong; 'and it is needful to our improved habits, that our roads and hedges, as well as every thing we have of a public nature, should correspond with our desires. Make a LABOUR FUND, and you will at once raise the spirit of the people of England, and place the merits of our institutions on their true footing: at all events, keep the poor-rates apart for pauper purposes.'

'Still,' replied Mr Blount, 'that would only be calling six half-a-dozen. There is a surplus population, or, in other words, a want of employment. How is that to be remedied?'

'By two ways – emigration and public works.'

'But where are the means to execute public works?'

'Circulation. Property must be taxed: the proceeds of this tax must be devoted to the employment of the labourers, for public advantage or ornament. From them the money will flow to the dealers, thence to those they employ, and so pervade the community.'

'But, Mr Diphthong,' quo' I, 'don't you see that the effect of that would be to bring down the large properties?'

'I do,' said he; 'but is not this better than to put an end to the rent of landlords, which is the present tendency of public opinion?'

'Really, Mr Diphthong, you put the matter in a very alarming light: is there no alternative?'

'I think not,' said he; 'the great properties have had their day: they are the relics of the feudal system, when the land bore all public burdens. That system is in principle overthrown, and is hastening to be so in fact. The system that it will be succeeded by is one that will give employment to the people – is one that will gradually bring on an equalisation of condition.'——

At this I started, for I saw by it that he was of the liberty and equality order; and grieved I was that men of his degree could talk so glibly on subjects that puzzle the highest heads in the land. But I said nothing: his sentiments, however, remain with me; and I cannot get the better of what he propounded about the feudal system being at an end, and of the system by which he thinks it is to be succeeded. Mr Blount was no less disturbed. We both agreed, that although Mr Diphthong was probably very wrong, something was going on in the world that gave a colouring to his inferences, and we concluded that a time was fast coming in which prudent and elderly men ought to quit the public arena, and leave it clear to the younger and the bolder. It was this conversation which in a great measure led me to think of retiring from Parliament.

CHAPTER XXXVI

Next week, when we returned to town, the first news we heard was, that the Duke's ministry were tottering, which I was much concerned to hear, as I thought the country at the time could ill spare such a straightforward man. My concern was the more deepened, as there was also a rumour, arising from the manifold fires and turbulence throughout the kingdom, that some change would be made in the way of a Reform of Parliament, to pacify the people.

The first report was not many days in circulation till it was confirmed; and sorry was I that the occasion chosen for doing it was one of a very insignificant kind. As the ministry had made up their minds to retire, it was, I must say, a weak and poor thing of them to make their resignation turn on the snuff-money of a few old shaking-headed dowagers. Surely it would better have become the Duke's manly nature to have given a frank and fair notice of his intention to break up his ministry, than to make it seem dissolved by the results of a question in the House that was not important.

The chief cause of my dissatisfaction was, however, in the event itself: for plain it was to me that the Duke's retiring from office, and the coming in of his adversaries, was a change amounting to something like a revolution. It was not, as other changes that had taken place before, a mutation of the Tory party among themselves, but a total renunciation of that ascendancy which they had so long preserved, and during which they had raised the country to the pinnacle of glory. I had, indeed, a sore heart when I saw the Whigs and Whiglings coming louping, like the puddochs of Egypt, over among the right-hand benches of the House of Commons, greedy as corbies and chattering like pyets. It was a sad sight; and I thought of the carmagnols of France, the honours of the Sitting, and all that which made our French neighbours, forty years ago, so wicked and ridiculous.

How I should have come to this conclusion concerning the new ministry and their abettors, requires no explanation. It was manifest to the humblest understanding that the Tories, our party, to whom the country owned so much both of renown and prosperity, were overthrown. We had for many years preserved the country, both from foreign and domestic foes; and every one must allow that we could not but feel greatly discomfited at being forced to abandon our supremacy to those who had never ceased, in all our illustrious career, to be the enemies of our enlightened policy.

No doubt, the Whigs in this revolution were the leaders; but they were backed and supported by a far stronger faction than themselves, – a faction who are looking forward to frighten them from their stools at the first expedient uproar of difficulty. It is, however, foreign to the principal purpose of this book, which is intended to let posterity know how those judicious supporters of Government felt and did like me, and who will, to a moral certainty, in the end be missed.

As soon as the new ministry had taken their places, I began, with the help of Mr Tough, to cast about for a gentleman to succeed me in the representation of Frailtown: but dealers were no longer rife. The rumour of the reform made purchasers shy; and though some there were who nibbled a little, he could find none that would bite, – so much did all the land stand in awe of this new phœnix which the ministry were known to be hatching.

When at last the plan did come out, I expected no better than a total loss by my seat; for although by it the power of representing two-and-twenty millions was proposed to be given to no less than the half of one million, it yet happened that Frailtown was included in the condemned list, the which I could not but think a very great hardship, and a most unjust thing, as the borough had been guilty of no misdemeanour to deserve such a punishment.

The other mischiefs of the measure troubled me very little. I saw that the die was cast, and that my wisest course was to make the best bargain I could for the borough, and retire by times to the Girlands, well aware that the one-and-twenty millions and a half will not be long content with such a fractional representation as it is proposed to give them; for what is the reform intended to do, unless it be to work out the abolition of rents and tithes? Less than that, I fear, will not satisfy the radicals; nor less than that, sooner or later, will a reform parliament, after it has again reformed itself, be found obliged to concede.

But I must not indulge these reflections, lest I be suspected of writing under feelings of disappointment and chagrin. The suspicion, indeed, would not, perhaps, be unfounded, for I acknowledge that I am vext; and no man has as yet greater reason, for just on the very day that Mr Tough had concluded a reasonable bargain with Mr Mysore, to succeed me in the representation of Frailtown, notice came out, that if the

Reform Bill did not pass, the Parliament would be dissolved, which caused him to draw back, and I could discover no other to take the seat off my hands. All the world knows the Parliament was dissolved, and my apprehended loss was in consequence inevitable.

It is true that Lord Dilldam wished me to stand again, upon the high Tory interest; but my moderation would not listen to the suggestion: indeed, his lordship shewed himself not very wise in this, for how could I expect to be well received in a town where my temperate politics were going out of fashion, the obstinate side? All was over; and to struggle I saw would be of no avail, so I determined, at the dissolution, to close my career, which I have accordingly done; and now, as a simple spectator, I look afar off for the coming on of what is ordained to take place.

THE END

NOTES

p. 1. *William Holmes:* Galt, at the outset, reinforces the 'authenticity' of his fictional hero Jobbry by having him dedicate his autobiography to a real person, William Holmes, M.P. from 1808 till 1832. D.N.B. describes him as 'the adroit and dexterous whip of the tory party . . . a most skilful dispenser of patronage'. Galt thus sets the stage for a picture of the operation of the system.

Colonel Napier: dedicated his history to Wellington 'because I have served long enough under your command to know, why the Soldiers of the Tenth Legion were attached to Caesar'.

your old office: i.e. of Tory whip.

p. 2. *a graduated property tax:* this form of income-tax, a war-time measure and a bad memory for the well-to-do, was not renewed by Parliament in 1816. Jobbry's fears that it would be re-introduced were justified.

Fulham: A contemporary route-book notes that Holmes had his residence in the rural village of Fulham (*Paterson's Roads*, ed. E. Mogg, 1822, p. 52).

p. 3. *a young friend:* a young relation. The Scots use of 'friend' for 'close relation' (husband, wife, cousin, etc.).

p. 4. *in Scotland:* Town Council delegates from the smaller Scottish boroughs (which were arranged for the purpose in 14 groups) elected a member for each group. There was plenty of scope for bribery and the solicitation of local and family connexions. But the open purchase of a seat from a sitting member (which is what Jobbry has in mind) was a simpler matter in England. See Porritt, *op. cit.*, on 'Seats acquired by Purchase', i, pp. 353ff.

a five-year old Parliament: One of the effects of the 1715 Septennial Act was to increase the cash-value of a seat, since the purchaser had an assured tenure for the seven year term. The canny Jobbry hopes for entry to the final two years of a parliament at a bargain price – and therefore a safe (and costless) seat.

cholera morbus: i.e. the 'plague' (of repairs).

p. 5. *the Indian directors:* directors of the East India Company (in Leadenhall Street).

p. 6. *Lord Entail:* as the major landholder in the district he controlled the election of both local members, (1) the 'county' M.P., who was elected by the freeholders, small property owners who were in their turn the creation of the Lord, and (2) the 'borough' M.P., who was elected by the three delegates of the grouped three borough councils – who in their turn were also 'under his thumb'. For another example see *The Provost*, chap. v.

freeholders: enfranchised small property owners. See above.

p. 7. *twelve hundred to fifteen hundred pounds per session:* Galt's figures are accurate. In 1807, fourteen hundred guineas a year was offered for a seat, in an advertisement in the *Morning Chronicle*. See Porritt, *op. cit.*, i, p. 358.

Ibbotson's Hotel: the London directories of the period (e.g. Holden's) list this hotel in Vere Street, Oxford Street.

p. 8. *according to Hoyle:* 'by the proper rules'. E. Hoyle's authoritative 'short treatises' on card games (especially his *Whist*, 1742) gave rise to the phrase.

p. 9. *at the Jerusalem . . . India House:* East India House was in Leadenhall Street. The nearby Jerusalem Coffee House (in Cowper's Court, Cornhill) was a 'subscription house for merchants and others trading to the East Indies', H. B. Wheatley, *London Past and Present*, 1891, ii, p. 308.

Carbonell's claret: London directories of the period list Carbonell and Son as wine-merchants in Golden Square, later in Regent Street.

p. 10. *Burns:* 'Tam o' Shanter', line 163.

man in a wig: i.e. the Speaker of the House of Commons. Jobbry is asking whether the member is expected to sit on the govenment or the opposition side of the House.

p. 11. *Smithfield:* even the cost of a trading-place at Smithfield meat-market is rising.

p. 13. *the true Simon Pure:* 'the genuine person'. A catch-phrase from Mrs Centlivre's *A Bold Stroke for a Wife*, 1717.

franks for letters: Members of Parliament had the privilege of free postage, by signing the outer cover of a letter. See note p. 79

p. 15. *petitioning:* Jobbry threatens to petition the House on the grounds of corrupt practices. See the following note.

contrary to law: though the purchase of seats remained common practice till 1832, it was contrary to an Act passed in 1809. See Porritt, *op. cit.*, i, p. 346. Jobbry is aware of both the actual law and the common practice – and can use either to his advantage.

p. 17. *reported progress . . . and asked leave to sit again:* an exclusively parliamentary expression, used of adjourning committee proceedings which are to be resumed later.

p. 18. *my constituents:* Jobbry slyly lets slip that *he* is the purchaser.

your offer: Probe accepts the gambit.

the Chiltern Hundreds: the legal fiction of being appointed to this 'office of profit under the King' (and so rendering oneself ineligible to be a Member of Parliament) is still the method of resigning one's seat. See Porritt, *op. cit.*, i, p. 242.

p. 20. *condescension:* Galt always (both in his published works and in his letters) uses this now pejorative word in the earlier (and neutral) sense 'voluntary abnegation of the privilege of superior rank' (O.E.D.).

the state fry: (fry: 'young fish') the younger members of noble families, with junior positions in the Government.

123

p. 20. *distributor of stamps:* one of the range of well-paid sinecures at the disposal of Government. Wordsworth's distributorship of stamps for Westmorland was worth about £500 a year in 1813 and later increased in value to about double this figure.

p. 23. *a canal:* the building of canals, requiring private Acts of Parliament, led to much lobbying for support among members. Galt himself, in 1819–20, had been well-paid as a parliamentary lobbyist by the Union Canal Company. See Gordon, *op. cit.,* p. 22.

p. 26. *gumflowers;* artificial flowers, used for hat-trimming.

p. 29. *operatives:* artisans.

p. 30. *Utilitarians:* followers of Jeremy Bentham. J. S. Mill (*Utilitarianism*) singles out Galt as having introduced the word to English usage.

p. 32. *Buonaparte:* the date is c. 1811–12.

p. 34. *Easyborough:* Galt's ironic name for a rotten borough.

p. 37. *ora rotundas:* 'eloquent voices'. From the Latin 'ore rotundo' ('with rounded phrase'), Horace *Ars Poet.,* 323. Galt's Irvine Grammar School education had given him a facility for Horatian tags. He wrote translations of some of the *Odes.*

pairing off: the parliamentary practice by which the whips arranged to set off the vote of a government absentee against that of an opposition absentee.

p. 38. *my daily franks:* abuse of the parliamentary privilege of free postage led to restrictions, in an Act of 1802; see Porritt, *op. cit.,* i, p. 288–9. A member in Jobbry's day was allowed ten franks a day, and the whole superscription (not merely the member's signature) on the 'cover' had to be in the member's handwriting – which explains Mr Gabblon's difficulties and the details of the ensuing scene.

p. 42. *my lodgings in Manchester Buildings:* a double row of private houses between Cannon Row and the Thames, a few hundred yards from the House 'principally occupied by bachelor members of parliament' (W. Thorby and E. Walford, *Old and New London,* 1873–8, iii, p. 381).

p. 43. *get to the north road:* Mr Tough orders the chaise to be driven south over the Thames by Westminster Bridge, then doubles back at the 'Obelisk' (where five roads converged in the Borough of Southwark), recrosses the river at Blackfriars Bridge, and resumes his original route north.

p. 45. *Athens of the north:* Edinburgh.

p. 47. *abstract one of the council:* Galt recounts a similar incident (based on actuality) in *The Provost,* chap. v.

p. 49. *a true bill:* Galt adds a further touch of 'authenticity'.

p. 54. *the Union:* Union of the Scottish and English Parliaments, 1707.

p. 56. *Lord Sidmouth:* Henry Addington, Prime Minister both at the time of the Treaty of Amiens (1802) and at the renewal of the war with the French (1803).

p. 58. *Abdiel:* the one faithful seraph (*Paradise Lost,* v, 896).

p. 59. *wally, wally:* i.e. 'lamentation' (from the ballad 'O waly waly').

Chaucer's pilgrims: the starting-point of the *Canterbury Tales* was the Tabard Inn in Southwark ('the Borough').

p. 60. *suffered . . . by an invasion of the enemy:* Mr Selby's situation was that of the Canadian settlers, ruined by the invasion of 1812, whom Galt represented for some years. See Gordon, *op. cit.,* p. 73.

p. 62. *Westminster:* franchise in this ancient 'scot and lot' borough was a function of residence and payment of municipal charges. The number of voters was consequently considerable (c. 17,000; see Oldfield, iv, p. 252) and elections were consequently Hogarthian.

p. 67. *three boroughs in the West:* Cornwall and Devon contained a very high proportion of the rotten boroughs abolished in 1832.

p. 73. *the plate:* wooden or metal tray carried by presbyterian elders gathering 'the collection' in church.

p. 77. *The multitude . . . to conserve their rights and privileges:* ironical – they had none.

p. 81. *tubs . . . to the whales:* i.e. 'diversionary tactics'. See O.E.D. and Swift's *Tale of a Tub,* Author's Preface.

p. 83. *balloted a member of a committee:* by the Grenville Act of 1770 charges of corruption at an election were determined by a committee of Members chosen by ballot. See Porritt, *op. cit.,* i, pp. 540–2.

Rhadamanthus: in Greek mythology, judge of the underworld.

p. 84. *freemen:* in essence, members of trade guilds. In many boroughs, the freeman had the preponderance of voting power and were able to enjoy 'the lucrative exercise of the franchise' (Porritt, *op. cit.,* i, p. 66).

p. 85. *The Melham bank . . . had stopped payment:* over sixty country banks failed in late 1825, as a result of over-issue of credit.

p. 87. *Colonel Armor:* a typical Galt 'cross-reference' to one of his other novels. He is a captain in *The Provost,* chap. xxix.

p. 88. *the Money Question:* during the war, gold had given way to paper currency. It was reintroduced in stages between 1820 and 1823, the pro's and con's being hotly debated in parliament and in the press.

p. 89. *paired off:* see note p. 37.

p. 90. *One night:* the ensuing 'night scene in London' was justly singled out for special praise by *Fraser's Magazine,* April 1832, pp. 373–4.

politician's pillow: Galt slyly hints that Jobbry's pillow has been shared in nights gone by – but the young woman of this night's encounter is very different.

p. 93. *a new canal:* see note p. 23.

potwalloper or freeholder: two of the varieties of enfranchised voters before 1832. A potwalloper was 'every inhabitant in the borough who had a family and boiled a pot there'; a freeholder – after the forty-shilling Act of 1430 – was a small property-owner. See Porritt, *op. cit.,* i, pp. 20, 31–2.

p. 96. *the Holy Alliance:* Alexander I of Russia's 'Christian' treaty of 1815, for which Jobbry professes admiration.

p. 98. *Machiavelli:* 'scheming politicians'. Galt (who had a competent knowledge of Italian) makes a mock-plural of the word. In 1814 he published an article based on his reading of Machiavelli. See Gordon, pp. 18, 50, 136.

Carbonari: secret society of republicans in Naples, formed in 1819 against the French occupation.

p. 99. *Catholic Relief Bill:* passed 1829.

p. 100. *rules . . . for the regulation of shipping:* relaxation and modification of the restrictive navigation laws were approved by the government in 1822 and on several later occasions.

p. 101. *Liberals:* the term had only recently become current in this sense. See O.E.D.

p. 102. *corn-laws:* originally passed to support and protect agriculture, they were resented by manufacturers and the town-workers (the 'operatives') and were subject to continual modification from 1815 onwards. Galt, though a Tory, personally supported the views of the manufacturers. See his article, 'Hints to the Country Gentlemen' in *Blackwood's Magazine*, October and November, 1822, where he adopts the persona of a Glasgow merchant.

p. 105. *George IV:* his death, 26 June 1830, resulted in an automatic dissolution of Parliament.

the Duke's party: i.e. the Tories, under the Duke of Wellington.

p. 107. *stramash:* riot (the Paris riots of July 1830, leading to the downfall of Charles X).

p. 109. *perfectibilians:* a relatively new coinage in Galt's day. O.E.D. credits Peacock (1816) with its first use.

p. 113. *Talbooth:* although Jobbry is brought before a magistrate in the south of England, he uses an exclusively Scottish term. In a small Scottish borough, the Tollbooth incorporated the Town Council offices, the magistrates' court, and the jail. See *The Provost*, chap. ix and elsewhere.

p. 116. *Mr Diphthong . . . on the poor-rates:* Mr Diphthong is expressing Galt's personal views, which he had already expounded (under a nom-de-plume) in 'Thoughts on the Times' in *Blackwood's Magazine*, October 1829, pp. 640–3. Galt – like Jobbry – was a 'moderate tory' but some of his personal political opinions were much more 'liberal' than Jobbry's.

p. 119, *the country owned so much:* 'the country acknowledged so great a debt'; 'owned' here is a Scotticism.

p. 120. *the condemned list:* the Schedule to the 1832 Act which contained the list of boroughs which would lose their right of electing members.

GLOSSARY

airt, direction.

anent, concerning.

arcana (Latin), secrets.

art or part (Scots Law), accessory.

a-trip (of an anchor), raised and ready to be 'weighed'.

auld farrent, 'old fashioned', experienced and wise.

bodie, person.

bum, hum, buzz.

by common, uncommon.

by times, betimes, in good time.

canny, artful, snug.

carle, old man.

carmagnol (French), revolutionary soldier.

cess, tax.

charming, 'chirming', chirping (of birds).

clanjamfrey, low worthless people; (hence) nonsense.

clok on, sit on (eggs), brood on.

cloots, hooves; (hence) feet.

cleek, clutch.

condescension. *See note* p. 20.

corbies, crows.

corruption, anger.

couthy, kindly.

daunering, strolling.

desjasket, dejected.

dungeon of wit, *phr.*, profound intellect.

enfeoffment (Scots law), possession.

enfeofft (Scots law), possessed.

erysipalis, inflammation.

ettarcap, spider, irascible person.

evendown, direct, blunt.

farm-steading, plot of farm land (also) farm-building.

fash, *sb. and v.*, trouble.

fashed, troubled.

Findhorn haddock, 'finnan haddock', smoke-cured haddock.

fozy, fat, stupid.

frank, privilege of free postage of letters by means of signature; a 'cover' so signed. *See note* p. 38.

friend, close relative (e.g. wife, husband, nephew. *See note* p. 3.

freeholder, elector deriving parliamentary franchise from freehold property. *See note* p. 93.

gaffer, elderly man.

gash, sharp, witty, shrewd.

gathering, savings, capital.

gruing, shivering.

gude son, son-in-law.

haffit, temple; 'thin haffits' – receding hair on the temples.

handling, dealing.

hithers and yons, 'to-ing and fro-ing' preliminary conversation not related to the real topic.

hobbletehoy, clumsy boy.

hogmanae, New Year's Eve.

hur, *sb.*, stir.

inns, inn.

invidia (Latin), envy.

jalouse, suspect.

laborious, *adj.*, labouring.

laddie, boy.

Little-good, the Devil.

loch, lake.

logive, extravagant.

louping, leaping.
ministerious, ministerial.
mobility, the common people.
morbus (Latin), sickness. *See note* p. 4.
o'ercome. 'burden' (of a song); recurring theme.
off-hand, plain-speaking.
operative, *sb.*, artisan, worker (esp. in mill or factory).
outcoming, surplus.
overly, *adv.*, too, too much.
pawkie, sly.
peuter. *vb.*, canvass for votes, solicit support.
plain stones, flat paving stones, 'pavement'.
plate. *See note* p. 73.
pockneuk, 'corner of a bag'; 'on my own pockneuk', on my ground.
potwalloper. *See note* p. 93.
pouking, plucking.
puddochs, frogs.
pyets, magpies.
quiscus, perplexing.
ramplor, roving, unsettled.
ree, drunken frenzy; 'on the ree' in a drunken frenzy.

sederunt (Latin), session.
shoon, shoes.
smock-frock, countryman's smock.
sneck-drawer, cunning expert; 'a manipulator of snecks' (door-latches).
sough, sound; 'with a calm sough', quietly.
souple, *supple*, cunning.
splore, skirmish.
spunk out, 'spark out', appear openly.
stane, stone.
steading, land for building, farmland, the buildings on the land.
stramash, riot, disturbance.
Talbooth, town-hall (which included the jail). *See note* p. 113.
tinkler, tinker, vagrant.
turnpike-house, toll-house on turnpike road.
upsetting, presumptious, ambitious.
vogie, cheerful.
waif, feeble.
wise, *vb.*, direct.
yird, earth, mud.